RIPE NOW:

A Haitian Congregation
Responds to the Great Commission

Frantz Lacombe

RIPE NOW: A Haitian Congregation Responds to the Great Commission
By Frantz Lacombe

Printed in the United States of America

VIGCOM Ministries
Frantz Lacombe
P.O. Box 2721
Des Plaines, IL 60017-2721
Tel: (847) 390-7156
www.vigcom.org

ISBN 0-9746487-0-1

Unless otherwise indicated, Bible quotations are taken from the New International Version Bible, Copyright © 1978 by the International Bible Society (IBS).

Cover design by Olivier Melnick, CA

Publication assistance through JoniwritrProductions
Huntington Beach, CA, JoniwritrProductions@iglide.net

Nouvelle Eglise Baptiste Missionnaire
1101 Church St. Evanston, IL 60201
Tel: (847) 424-8809

Fidlar Doubleday

Early Response to *RIPE NOW*

This thesis is a challenge to me personally; I have been influenced by the missionary approach of Donald McGravan that reminds us that a church grows better or even faster within a homogeneous milieu. Over the past 30 years, I have developed a 100 percent ethnic Haitian church; my ministry has been horizontal, reaching only Haitians worldwide. Now this book (the thesis) challenges me to reach out beyond the Haitian borders, into the whole world. I [earnestly hope] it will spark a new fire in the heart of every Haitian leader.
Dr. Soliny Vedrine, International Coordinator, Global Vision of Protestantism in the Haitian Milieu.

Pastor Lacombe's treatise of the application of the Great Commission in the Haitian Church at large could not have come at a more opportune time. The book *RIPE NOW* will open new vistas to pastors, church members, and layworkers in the missions field in Haiti and abroad. **Carl Vancol, M.D.**

Pastor Lacombe places a figurative stethoscope on the Haitian Church (the churches in Haiti as well as Haitian churches in other countries) to check its health and vitality. His diagnosis, in the area of carrying out the Great Commission (found in Acts 1:8), finds the church ailing. The results of this ailment are apparent. It is a church apparently healthy, vital, and witnessing at home but is a wheezing, asthmatic, breathless church failing to bear witness to the rest of the world. Pastor Lacombe states that the restricted missionary vision of the Haitian Church is due in part to people living in poverty not being able to imagine traveling to other regions of the world. Pastor Lacombe had over a hundred Haitians fill out a survey about their understanding of and willingness to obey the Great Commission. The responses are strikingly honest and thought-provoking. This survey "self test" is a challenging example to all believers that we must occasionally examine our current practices and beliefs to see if they comply with biblical teaching. Pastor Lacombe offers a prescription for the ailing Haitian Church…He has offered an exciting variety of practical suggestions for helping believers repair their ailing ideas about the Great Commission. These remedies are like a breath of fresh air.
Robert L. Schultz, Former missionary to Niger and France with EBM.

Historically, many Haitian churches are suffering spiritually due to a truncated vision for global missions. This sober reality demands an urgent response from the religious community. Pasteur Lacombe has embraced the critical task of wrestling with this problem, reflecting his passion for a globally-oriented church. In addition to prayerful preparation and excellent research, Rev. Lacombe has laboriously invested in creating practical proposals that would transform the Haitian Church's philosophy of missions. He is to be commended for a work that has drawn special attention to a spiritual disease that is plaguing the Body of Christ. Following well-argued conclusions and recommendations, this keen author has generated a wealth of comprehensive materials for a church seeking to flourish in its vision for missions. In conclusion, this thesis, which merits a broader context for expression, proves to be an invaluable resource for the contemporary Haitian Church. **Margery Berthole, Th.M., Dallas Theological Seminary.**

Pastor Frantz Lacombe has a heart for missions. He always wanted to see the Haitian Church and [its] leaders involved in overseas mission fields. With this book, *Ripe Now*, he is trying to challenge Haitian leaders and their congregations to reach people beyond the [boundaries of Haiti]. **Pastor, Evangelist, Matthieu Jean Baptiste, President and Founder of HECA (Haitian Evangelical Crusade Association).**

Doing missions in the Haitian churches has long been a neglected Command. This responsibility falls squarely on the pastor's shoulders. He is the cheerleader; he is the influencer; he is supposed to point the Church in the Lord's direction. Secondly, it is the pastor's responsibility to train and equip the members of the Church so they can carry out the Great Commission. If not, we are simply playing church and not impacting the world for Christ. *RIPE NOW: A Haitian Congregation Responds to the Great Commission*, is a must-read for all Haitian pastors. It will put us back on the track the Lord intended for us to be on. **Pastor Mullery Jean Pierre Eglise Baptiste Beraca, Brooklyn, NY.**

The pastors have ceased to preach on the Great Commission. With *RIPE NOW*, everyone will be able to catch up. This book is written from the hands of a man of God, Pastor Frantz Lacombe, whose thoughts have been directed by God for his thesis. *RIPE NOW* is an indispensable tool for churches that would like the Great Commission to become a turning point in their lives, particularly in the Haitian churches. **Marie Myrtha Eleazard, Former missionary to Réunion with AIM.**

This thesis is an excellent work on The Great Commission, a subject that should impact both Haitian churches and other ones. The author's enthusiasm for missions is contagious...He uses the Bible to explain the deep meaning and implication of the Great Commission...Advancement in global missions by Haitians is encouraging, as documented in Lacombe's work, perhaps the best source available for such information. Despite the influence of Christian Western worldviews in *RIPE NOW* (the thesis), the [author's] solutions (themselves Western in philosophy and methodology)...to improve the global application of the Great Commission (Western expression) among Haitian believers are excellent and recommendable. **Frantz S. Morisset: Coordinateur Exécutif, Vision Globale.**

Haitian churches are going through a period of rapid growth but also of social, economic, and cultural flux. A new "**missionary vision**" for this church is presently a real concern. We do understand that the Great Commission does not stop with preaching the gospel...I believe that the purpose of this book (research project) is to provide a planning path for the Haitian Church to develop, affirm, and communicate [its] vision for fulfilling Christ's mission in all the communities God calls [it] to serve. This work combines factual examination of current forces at work with penetrating evaluation of the Haitian Church's past, present, and potential effectiveness. Since it is Radio Lumiere's expressly stated goal to serve all the evangelical churches, leaders, and pastors of Haiti in the area of continuing Christian education, the work of Frantz Lacombe is for us a complement and a powerful contribution toward the fulfillment of the overall goals of the National Church. It is my sincere hope that Haitian churchmen might find *RIPE NOW: A Haitian Congregation Responds to the Great Commission* (based on his thesis, "Communicating a Missionary Vision to the Haitian Church According to the Mandate of the Great Commission") to be an instrument that helps their churches make new strides for the sake of the Kingdom. **Varnel Jeune, General Director, Radio Télé-Lumière, Haiti.**

Mission is the Church in action. A church cannot be effective without a missionary vision, and it also loses its spiritual vitality. The piece of work you have presented under the title *RIPE NOW* ("Communicating a Missionary Vision to the Haitian Church") stimulates action, [and] encourages me to continue with the missionary vision...It involves the Great Commission given by the Lord...Without the fulfillment of this command, the church is sterile and fails to comprehend the objective for which it came into being...Rev. Lacombe, this wonderful work you have presented...has given me the understanding that no one can be a true Christian and be exempt from the responsibility in the mission ministry....You have a clear conviction not only of the mission given to the Haitian Community, but also of the call given to you. **Dr. Jamil Georgeon, Senior Pastor, Eglise Baptiste du Rédempteur d'Expression Francaise (Brooklyn).**

The Great Commission did not leave anybody out. By giving it as His last command, our Lord has shown us the importance of always remembering our responsibility, as His Church, to the home front, to the ends of the earth, and to everywhere in between! While we are indeed to share God's love within our own families and cultures, we will also need to recognize and accept [the] fact that we are now part of a world-wide family, and that this family will one day be composed of those of every tribe and nation. Jews, Greeks, barbarians, wise and unwise, male and female are all justified one way and one way only, and our own people are not the exception...It will always be necessary to teach our children and new believers the Great Commission in all its aspects and to constantly check our priorities against it, both as individuals and as communities of believers. If I don't love my neighbor next door, it will be hard for me to love my neighbor when I get off the plane in the Congo. **Rosemary Walker, Regional Coordinator with AIM Canada.**

For generations, the Christians in Haiti and elsewhere have been unaware of their personal responsibility for fulfilling the Great Commission. Because of this oversight, the Church in Haiti has not been able to reach its full potential. Through the guidance of the Holy Spirit and many hours of research, Pastor Lacombe has compiled an eye-opening, comprehensive evaluation that traces why this tragedy has permeated the entire Haitian Church. The lessons contained in the study have the potential to bring change as the church embraces the global vision of the Great Commission. If it is done properly, the Haitian churches in Haiti and abroad can become a vital force in changing the world for Christ. **Janette Lazer, Former missionary to Alaska with Interact Mission.**

The true purpose for which the Church exists is to make disciples, to bring reconciliation, and to establish a new communion..."Communicating a Mission Vision to the Haitian Church According to the Mandate of the Great Commission" is the responsibility that Pastor Frantz Lacombe has given to himself in this research. It is the first missiological research about this [subject]....I recommend this research without reservation. **Dr. Elie D. Weick, Senior Pastor of French District, Lake Region Conference of SDA Church.**

The Evangelical Church of Haiti has come a long way. [Coming] mostly from a rural and peasant church with the pioneer missionaries, it has made some significant strides as a whole and [inroads of] progress into the Haitian society. But a deeper inside look and a careful analysis by Pastor Frantz Lacombe have revealed a shocking diagnosis: It is a church plagued with a very dangerous disease -- some type of a short-sighted and defective missionary vision -- that cripples her [from fully embracing] the biblical mandate as being outlined in the Great Commission. Fully aware that the present is often a reflection of the past, the author has skillfully and painstakingly labored in order to provide a very scientific and objective historical overview of various missionary works, seeking to unearth the underlying factors that cause the illness in the first place. [He] then moves on to present some practical insights in terms of recommendations. At the outset of the twenty-first century, when missions agencies/societies are reviewing their policies and methods, the timing cannot be more right for such a needed and long-awaited tool, most likely the first of its kind. I highly and ardently recommend this book to missionaries, Christian leaders, Bible schools, and seminary students. **Pastor Pierre Cadet, Missionary to Haiti with EBM.**

...Honor, power, and glory are to Our Great God for His deeds. The Great Commission — the hope of mankind. **Frère Bien-aimé Jeanty, Eglise Haitienne de la Grâce, CMA**

ABOUT THE COMPANION WEB SITE

To extend and complete your learning experience about the Great Commission, we invite you to visit our companion website at www.vigcom.org.

Read *RIPE NOW: A Haitian Congregation Responds to the Great Commission.*

Encourage pastors, deacons, Bible schools, seminaries, laypeople, and the Haitian churches in Haiti and abroad to embrace the vision of the Great Commission wholeheartedly because "It is more blessed to give than to receive." (Acts 20:35)

Pray that God would raise up an army of Haitian Missionaries who will be willing to take the gospel to the nations of the world.

Support VIGCOM Ministries through individual or corporate membership in order to bring the Haitian churches in Haiti and overseas to the next level, enabling more to make a contribution to the fulfillment of the Great Commission worldwide.

Log on and take the free, interactive quiz developed by VIGCOM Ministries. The quiz results will help you uncover your strengths and weaknesses when it comes to catching the vision of the Great Commission. You will also find suggestions for ways to further develop your personal and corporate missions.

We hope you enjoy the book and the website, and we trust that you will embrace the global vision of the Great Commission as spelled out in the Gospels and Acts and be empowered to reach the world for Christ.

VIGCOM Ministries
P.O. Box 2721, Des Plaines, IL 60017-2721
Tel : (847) 390-7156
www.vigcom.org

VIGCOM Ministries Membership Application Form

Important - Incomplete applications will not be processed.

You may use this form to apply in your name, or for your ministry, your church or a para-church organization. Please indicate whether you are applying individually or for an organization. Application does not guarantee automatic membership. VIGCOM Ministries reserves the right to accept or refuse any applicant who does not meet all the requirements.

Applicant Information

Section I. Personal Information
Last Name: _____ First Name: _____ Middle: _____
Address_____
City and State_____ Zip Code _____
Sex:_____ Title:_____ Your Email:_____
Tel: (_____) _____ - _____ Date:_____

Section II. Organization Information
Are you applying for yourself or for an organization?
Yourself____, an Organization_____ or Both_____

For Organizations:
Organization's Name:_____
Address _____
City and State_____ Zip Code _____
Tel:_____ Email:_____
Person in charge:_____

Name of your church: _____
Address: _____

Section III. Membership Fees
Becoming an individual or corporate member of VIGCOM Ministries will help you connect to a network of resources for your walk with God and for use by your family, community, and church, to facilitate getting the message of salvation out both to Haitians and the nations of the world in every imaginable way. Your membership will offer you access to additional information that is not available to the greater public (through the internet), and will give you discounts, (as posted) on products supported by this ministry. Please indicate the desired extent of your annual membership:
Individual: 1 yr ____ ($30), 2 yrs___ ($55), 5 yrs___ ($130), 10 yrs_____ ($250)
Corporate: 1 yr ___ ($100), 2 yrs___ ($190), 5 yrs___ ($475), 10 yrs _____ ($900)

(continued on reverse side)

I affirm that my statements above and in the attached pages are correct to the best of my knowledge. Also, if admitted to VIGCOM Ministries, I agree to abide by the standards of conduct of VIGCOM Ministries.

Applicant Signature: _____Date:_____

Please mail this membership application form to the address below:
VIGCOM Ministries
P.O.BOX 2721
DES PLAINES, IL 60017-2721

Reserved for Office Use Only

Date Received:_____ Date Processed:_____ Decision:_____
Name:_____ Signature:_____
Date:_____

RIPE NOW:
A Haitian Congregation Responds to the Great Commission

Book Order Form

Name: _____

Mailing Address: _____

_____

City: _____ State:_____ Zipcode:_____

Telephone #: _____ Email Address: _____

Book Quantity: _____ @ $15.99 US or 23.99 Canadian_____
Membership Discount: _____

Shipping and Handling: _____
($3.00 per book US or $4.00 per book CAN)

Total for this order: $_____

You can pay by credit card (Visa, Mastercard, American Express, ATM Debit card), check or cash. Make checks payable to:
VIGCOM Ministries
P.O.BOX 2721
Des Plaines, IL 60017-2721
Visit our website: www.vigcom.org

Thank you for your interest and support!

ABSTRACT

This paper grew out of a thesis project concerning the limited missionary vision of the Haitian Church. That led the author to study afresh the Great Commission, which is the global vision commanded by Jesus Christ to His Church, as recorded in the Gospels and Acts.

There was also a need to uncover the causes and effects of the limited vision in the Haitian Church in Haiti and abroad. The literature reviewed unearthed that, in spite of impressive numerical growth, the animistic context embedded in a Voodoo worldview had been ignored by those who communicated the gospel message in Haiti. As a result of their underlying worldview, Haitian believers typically ended up reaching out only to their own people, and thus their worldview impeded their process of reaching the world for Christ.

In an attempt to correct this limited vision, many Haitian pastors and laypeople helped refine a survey that was distributed to Haitian believers during a pretest held in Chicago, Illinois, on February 23, 2002. One hundred and nine surveys out of a total of 115 were returned. The interpretation of the results of this survey supported the hypothesis that men, women, and even the younger generation of Haitians in Chicago have a different understanding of the Great Commission than that advanced by the Gospel writers. For many congregants, missions is a confusing concept equated with hospital or jail visitation and compassion ministries.

This document concludes that five factors seem to limit the vision of the Haitian Church, and three recommendations are made to remedy the situation. The first recommendation focuses on the way the gospel was brought to Haitians. The second focuses on the way the gospel was received by the Haitians. The last recommendation focuses on church members' current understanding of the Great Commission. As a result of applying these recommendations, the New Missionary Baptist Church (NMBC) caught the vision of supporting four missionary couples in a period of two years: one Haitian, one American, one Jewish and one Korean. In addition, a young woman committed her life to serve as a missionary in a cross-cultural setting. Therefore, the NMBC is living proof that the Great Commission in its global perspective, as commanded by Jesus, is achievable by the Haitian Church in Haiti and abroad.

H

To my God,
to Whom all the credit is due.

Meanwhile, the disciples were urging Jesus to eat. "No," he said, "I have some food you don't know about."

"Who brought it to him?" the disciples asked each other.

Then Jesus explained: "My nourishment comes from doing the will of God who sent me, and from finishing his work. Do you think the work of harvesting will not begin until the summer ends four months from now? Look around you! Vast fields of human souls are ripening all around us, and are ready now for reaping. The reapers will be paid good wages and will be gathering eternal souls into the granaries of heaven! What joys await the sower and the reaper, both together! For it is true that one sows and someone else reaps. I sent you to reap where you didn't sow; others did the work, and you received the harvest." John 4:31-38 (The Living Bible)

ACKNOWLEDGEMENTS

Seven years' journey in Academia requires grace, perseverance, and commitment. This ongoing thesis project is the culmination of those years at Moody Graduate School. Such research is rarely the product of one single person, and this project is no exception. Many people have in one way or another contributed to this paper through prayer, counsel, encouragement, challenge, special assistance, and in many other ways. Unfortunately, due to lack of space, the author cannot list everyone.

Thanks to my primary advisor Dr. Marvin Newell for his understanding and flexibility that made the project more enjoyable than burdensome. Thanks to my advisor Dr. Michael McDuffee who inspired me to believe in the feasibility of this project. Thanks to Dr. Bill Thrasher who fervently prayed for me, and to Dr. Dan Green who taught me how to do biblical theology.

Thanks to the members of the New Missionary Baptist Church who supported me in so many ways. Thanks to the VIGCOM core group for their devotion, investment, and sacrifice (Pressoir, Tamie, and Lyvie Belance; Yanick Remé, Iramène Juline, and Kettia St-Paul). Thanks to my parents Franck and Agathe Lacombe for their constant prayers as well as my beloved sister Yolette Jeune. Thanks to my brothers:Raymond Lother, Tessier, Bonard, Fredzer, and Thierry for their continual support and to Dr. Hebert Lacombe who critiqued the document and challenged my thinking.

Thanks to Pastor Pierre R. and Yvette Cadet for their friendship. Thanks to Dr. Chavannes Jeune for his great contribution to this work. Thanks to Dr. Fritz Fontus, Dr. Soliny Vedrine, Dr. Thomas Jean Baptiste, Dr. Claude Noel, Dr. Jules Casséus, Pastor Edner Jeanty, Pastor Matthieu J. Baptiste, Pastor J. Lilite, Pastor Brezil St-Germain, Marie M. Eleazard, Jan Lazer, Rosemary Walker for her sacrifice, Lau Chi, Robert Schultz for his devotion, Dr. Jamil Georgeon, Dr. Elie Weick,

Dr. Rolland Joachin, Frantz Morissett, and Edwin Walker for letting me use the unpublished materials, and to all who reviewed and critiqued the manuscript. Thanks to David Mays for granting permission to use his CD-ROM, to Joseph Cataio for his support, to Dr. David Haag for his godliness, and to Holly Schmidt and Tiffany Peeler for retreat accommodations.

Thanks to Dr. Carl Vancol, Raymond Noel, Claude Jean Baptiste, and (again) to my assistant secretary Kettia Saint-Paul for their strong desire and commitment to anticipate changes in the Haitian Community at large.

Thanks to Margery Berthole for her valuable input, to Olivier Melnick and family for their hospitality, love, and the design of the book cover, to my editor Joni Prinjinski for her constant encouragement and for making this book more enjoyable to read. Thanks to all the people at Fidlar DoubleDay who worked so hard to get this book out on time and did such a fine job.

Finally, thanks to my Lord and Savior Jesus Christ, Who never gives up on me, has entrusted me with such an important topic so dear to Him, and has given me the determination, passion, and stamina to finish the work. May this book please Him as it brings honor and glory to His Holy Name alone.

TABLE OF CONTENTS

LIST OF FIGURES

FOREWORD

This book is a great contribution to the Haitian Church as we approach the celebration of Haiti's 200 years of independence! I truly believe deep in my heart that this book is not an accident, and simply neither an academic paper nor a mere intellectual exhibit just for the sake of presenting a thesis in partial fulfillment of the requirements of the Master of Divinity. Instead, as the author, Rev. Frantz Lacombe, puts it in his own words, it grew out of a concern that the missionary vision of the Haitian Church is definitely restricted, not to say lacking.

Inspired by academic growth, his ecclesiastical practice, and his burden for souls, Pastor Lacombe began questioning me about this subject almost five years ago. As a missiologist and former President of the Evangelical Baptist Mission of Southern Haiti (MEBSH) with expertise in this environment, I had long been interested in missions and had a strong ambition to see the Haitian Church reach new heights. Thus I, along with other missionaries, provided information to help Rev. Frantz Lacombe better understand the problematic of missions in the Haitian Church, both in Haiti and abroad. I consider this book, RIPE NOW, presents both theological and scientific approaches to finding solutions. The theological part is a response intended to remedy the weaknesses relating to missionary activities in our churches, while the scientific part reveals the need to train the Haitian leaders and educate born-again Haitian believers.

It has been five years since Rev. Frantz Lacombe and I, along with several other Haitian missiologists, began reflecting on this important issue without being able to table in writing the causes and effects of such a limited vision in the Haitian Church despite the phenomenal numerical growth over the last fifteen years in our churches both inside Haiti and overseas.

Out of this great burden, Rev. Lacombe has designed a survey, which has been refined by laypeople and leaders and then conducted among some 115 people in the Chicago area. Who could have thought that this survey would actually serve as the most feasible data collection instrument in preparation of this more-than-needed document at the turn of this new century of Haiti history?

After 511 years (1492-2003) of Haitian missions history, and 187 years (1816-2003) of Protestant history in Haiti, there is no doubt that the investigation of an issue such as a limited vision of the Great Commission in the Haitian Church is quite a challenge. Pastor Lacombe not only takes the challenge, but also devotes himself to tackling the root causes by identifying five key factors which seem to limit the vision of the Haitian Church. He then goes one step further by making three recommendations to remedy the situation. The first recommendation has to do with *the way the gospel was brought to Haitians.* The second recommendation aims at *the way the gospel was received by the Haitians.* The last recommendation focuses *on church members' understanding of the Great Commission.*

Pastor Lacombe has moved to model or apply his recommendations in his own church setting, which really led him to believe that the Great Commission in its global perspective is achievable in the Haitian Church at large.

So much time, energy, and money have been spent in buying buildings and securing lands for the sake of expanding our ministries, while the Great Commission is yet to be fulfilled. Don't we understand the time is Ripe for the harvest? The church of Jesus Christ in Haiti more than ever before is called to a new mandate: "Claim Haiti for Christ and Christ for Haiti." May this book *RIPE NOW: A Haitian Congregation Responds to the Great Commission* challenge each of us in this crucial time of our history so that the Haitian Church rises up to the Biblical mandate of the Great Commission.

In the spirit of the recommendations of this book, we want to see the churches in Haiti develop new strategies and reorder their priorities so as to reach, wherever they are planted, all the ethnic groups and people of other nations. We have been so long confined to only reaching people within our own nation and cultural setting. The time is RIPE to look beyond our cultural barriers and geographical boundaries. The time is RIPE for the

Haitian Church to grow not only Christian people, but world-class Christian citizens. This is the plea of this book.

What a tremendous step in modeling not only a great vision but, equally, an obligation of the entire Church of Jesus Christ. It is our wish and prayer that this book will serve its purpose and objective; that is, to motivate National leaders and churches alike to participate in the fulfillment of the Great Commission worldwide.

It is also our hope and desire that, moreover, local missions in Haiti, seminaries, and Bible schools would look forward to using the findings in this book in their curricula and leadership training as well as in Bible study groups and Sunday schools.

May God continue to inspire men and women likewise who will be reading this book to see the need of a global view of the Great Commission, and may He help the churches in Haiti and abroad to shift their focus to a universal view of the missionary mandate as stated by the author in his study objectives.

Rev. Chavannes Jeune
October 9, 2003
New York

PREFACE

Two relentless questions have dawned on me for years as a pastor ministering primarily to the Haitian community. Why are some American Protestant churches so devoted to the fulfillment of the Great Commission worldwide while the Haitian church in Haiti and abroad finds the concept of the Great Commission to be an abstract reality? How can the author be used by the Lord to bring a contribution to the Haitian churches at the dawn of the third Century celebration of Haiti's independence? Through groaning and persistent prayer, I sought an answer from God. He answered both questions as I was taking a course entitled "Seminar of Church History" at Moody Graduate School. In this book, I share with you what I learned, through prayer, study, research, analysis, and application.

I recognize some restrictions in terms of the scope of my research. The activities of many denominations, leaders, churches, and organizations in Haiti and abroad could not be represented in this work due to inaccessibility of data. Though the data collected were largely representative of the Haitian churches in Haiti and abroad, nonetheless the interpretation of the pivotal survey is applicable particularly to the New Missionary Baptist Church (NMBC) in Evanston, Illinois. This small sampling suggested that there is much more that can be explored in a project of the magnitude of encouraging the Haitian church at large to respond more fully to the Great Commission. Now my burning desire is to see the Lord open new doors of opportunity to bring this study to another level for His glory and for the sake of the Haitian churches in Haiti and abroad.

In retrospect, there is a genuine sense of appreciation to God and to those who invested their lives for the advancement of the gospel in Haiti. Nonetheless, nothing could be more fitting than George Santayana's statement: "Those who cannot remember the past are condemned to repeat it." In essence, the intent of this paper is twofold: first, to explore the factors that contributed to impeding the vision of the Haitian churches in Haiti and abroad and, secondly, to formulate recommendations to remedy the situation to the glory of the Lord and Savior Jesus Christ.

INTRODUCTION:
AN APPROACH TO
FOCUSING OUTWARD

"The harvest is so great, and the workers are so few," he [Jesus] told his disciples. "So pray to the one in charge of the harvesting, and ask him to recruit more workers for his harvest fields." Matthew 9:37-38 (The Living Bible)

H

The Great Commission is one of the most important motifs in the entire Bible. Its importance is seen by its location, content, significance, purpose, and scope within the Bible. The Great Commission is associated with the very nature of God and clarifies for us His program for the world and His Church.

The idea of the Great Commission is alive and well today. Currently, the Great Commission is discussed on the worldwide web, in contemporary books and journals as well as by scholars, theologians, pastors, students, and lay people in the settings of schools, churches and para-church organizations. Nonetheless, differences in applicability and interpretation have created a sense of confusion regarding how the Great Commission is to be carried out.

From an historical perspective, the Church has sometimes embraced and at other times overlooked the Great Commission, both in teaching and in practice. While the Church was born in a wave of missionary fervor, the sense of urgency of making disciples (instead of merely converts) waned until the time of the Reformation (Moreau 2002, 412). Although serious interest in applying the Great Commission recurs from time to time, the Church has still not fully regained a sense of the importance of its mission in the world.

An example of this loss of urgency became clear to me as I examined the Haitian Missionary Church (HMC) in Evanston, Illinois, where I am pastor. As a native Haitian, I had observed for

1

many years the disparity between the limited missions vision of Haitian churches and the activities of some American churches, especially compared to American Evangelical churches. I began to analyze this serious problem in the life and vision of this church by attempting to state the problem, define key terms, and discover the significance of the Great Commission through Bible study and prayer. As I began my study, I researched the theological and biblical basis of the study and made note of the study limitations and the basic assumptions I had to make.

After outlining my approach, I reviewed relevant literature related to past missions work in Haiti and conducted interviews with selected missionaries, pastors, local mission leaders, and seminary students with the purpose of answering this question: *What factors may help explain a limited vision of the missionary mandate in the Haitian Church?* I then designed a survey to use with respondents from my local church to assess their understanding of the Great Commission. I designed the questionnaire so that I would be able to interpret the data according to age group and gender.

After analyzing the results from the survey, I came to some conclusions about roadblocks we at the HMC were facing, and I made some concrete recommendations for overcoming these obstacles in our own small congregation. I believe these results may have broader implications for other congregations.

Getting to the Root of the Problem

Anyone who understands the importance of the Great Commission in God's agenda and is acquainted with the Haitian Church would most likely raise this same question: *Why are Haitian churches (both in Haiti and abroad) generally uninvolved in overseas missions.* The HMC, my small congregation, may be used as a paradigm for the purpose of investigating this limitation.

When I planted the HMC in 1996, the primary goal for the ministry was to impart a missionary vision to the congregation. That vision was to proclaim the gospel message in order to bring non-believers into a dynamic relationship with the Lord and Savior Jesus Christ and to equip them to become mature disciples in their faith (Matthew 28:19-20; Ephesians 4:11-15). With this in mind, we inserted the word "missionary" into the church's name to indicate the direction of the church. Overall, the congregation was to maintain its Haitian cultural heritage, but at the same time, many activities were designed to focus the attention of the church on missions.

Although the congregation at HMC attempted to expand its horizon on missions, it took about three years for members to realize that they had an *internal*, rather than an *external*, focus for their thinking and activities. This growing awareness became possible through the training I received as a pastor attending Moody Graduate School and participating in Sonlife Ministries.

My new training helped me examine the structure of the HMC in light of the global aspect of the Great Commission. I realized that we individually and corporately had a limited view of the missionary mandate. From that moment, I felt the urgent necessity of communicating to my church a missionary vision congruent with the Great Commission.

One activity that came to have a high impact on focusing the vision of the HMC was an annual missions conference that we initiated at our congregation. Each year the congregation invited missionaries from Haiti and the United States to be part of its missions conference.

In 1999, the Lord allowed the church to have its first missions trip to Haiti. In 2001, the congregation commissioned a Haitian family of seven to be missionaries in partnership with Evangelical Baptist Missions (EBM) and other Baptist churches in the United States. In 2002, an American couple was commissioned by the church to be in missionary partnership with Heart of God Ministries (HGM) and other Evangelical churches in the United States. Subsequent to their commission by HMC, both the Haitian and American families were sent out to serve the Lord in Haiti, in 2001 and 2002 respectively.

In 2003, the church looked at the possibility of supporting two other missionary families in cross-cultural settings outside Haiti:

one in California working with Chosen People Ministries (CPM) and another in the Republic of Guinea (West Africa) with Teach us Missions (TM). Another missionary going to France (Europe) is currently on the waiting list for support in 2004.

By 2003, HMC had allocated approximately 20 percent of its budget for missions to support their commissioned missionaries in Haiti and abroad and their own missions activities within the congregation.

The remainder of the paper deals with the methodology of addressing the issue of changing from an inward to an outward focus at the local congregation level. I undertook a personal study of the theological and biblical basis of the Great Commission, which follows in chapter 1. I also developed a detailed description of a vision for global missions, which the reader will find in chapter 5.

The following are working definitions that furnish common ground for communicating this approach for expanding missions activities within congregations of believers.

Working Definitions

Animism: "The belief that personal spiritual beings and impersonal spiritual forces have power over human affairs and, consequently, that human beings must discover what beings and forces are influencing them in order to determine future action and, frequently, to manipulate their power" (Van Rheenen 1991, 20).

Charismatics: "Those who testify to a renewing experience of the Holy Spirit and present exercise of the gifts of the Spirit such as glossalalia, healing, prophecy and miracles" (Johnstone and Mandryk 2001, 755).

Church (with a capital C): "A particular denomination or the universal visible Church at a national or worldwide level" (Johnstone and Mandryk 2001, 755).

church (with a small c): "A local fellowship of believers. The word is commonly used to mean a church building or church service, but in this study this usage has largely been avoided" (Johnstone and Mandryk 2001, 755).

Communicating: Transmitting information to another person or a group of people in their cultural context so that the message is accurately received and understood.

Contextualization: A mode of communication that involves utilizing the worldview of the host culture to provide a framework for the questions and needs of that people and as a guide to the emphasis of the message; the cultural gifts of that people become the medium of expression. This means of cross-cultural communication aims to be faithful to Scripture and relevant to culture[1]. (Moreau 2000, 225, 245)

Culture: "The more or less integrated systems of ideas, feelings, and values and their associated patterns of behavior and products shared by a group of people who organize and regulate what they think, feel, and do" (Hiebert 2001, 30). (Also, see appendix 1 for diverse definitions of culture.)

Evangelicals (with capital E): "All who generally emphasize: the Lord Jesus Christ as the sole source of salvation through faith in Him; a personal faith and conversion with regeneration by the Holy Spirit; a recognition of the inspired Word of God as the only basis for faith and Christian living; a commitment to biblical witness, evangelism and mission that brings others to faith in Christ" (Johnstone and Mandryk 2001, 756).

Evangelism: "The activity of Christians spreading the gospel" (Johnstone and Mandryk 2001, 756).

Evangelization: "The process of proclaiming the gospel globally or regionally" (Johnstone and Mandryk 2001, 756).

Gospel (with capital G): The four books of the New Testament which gave an account of Jesus Christ's ministry, life, death and resurrection.

gospel (with a small g): The good news of Jesus Christ's ministry, life, death, resurrection, ascension, and His return.

Great Commission: The final command Jesus gave to His disciples to preach the gospel and make disciples of all nations (Matthew 28:18-20; Mark 16:15-16; Luke 24:46-48; John 20:21; Acts 1:8).

---

[1]In another way, contextualization parallels the general sense of inculturation which refers to "the incarnation of Christian life and of the Christian message in a particular cultural context, in such a way that this experience not only finds expression through elements proper to the culture in question, but becomes a principle that animates, directs and unifies the culture, transforming and remaking it so as to bring about 'a new creation.'" (Moreau 2000, 475- 476)

Haitian Church: An Evangelical church of Afro-Caribbean makeup only or mixed, in Haiti or abroad.

Haitian Missionary Church (HMC): Refers to an Evangelical Baptist church located in Evanston, Illinois.

Mission: According to George Peters "a comprehensive term including the upward, inward and outward ministries of the church: The church as 'sent' (a pilgrim, stranger, witness, prophet, servant, as salt…) in this world" (Moreau 2000, 637).

Missionary: In general, "one who is sent with a message[2]" (Johnstone and Mandryk 2001, 757).

Missionary Mandate: Synonymous with the Great Commission in this study.

Missionary Vision: A global vision that seeks to bring a contribution to the fulfillment of the Great Commission through the proclamation of the gospel both locally and cross-culturally and to make disciples of all nations according to the teaching and the command of the Lord Jesus Christ.

Missions: According to C. Gordon Olson: "the whole task, endeavor, and program of the Church of Jesus Christ is to reach out across geographical and/or cultural boundaries, by sending missionaries to evangelize people who have never heard or who have little opportunity to hear the saving gospel" (Olson 1993, 13).

Non-Western world: "The countries of Latin America, Africa and Asia. Rarely have we used the synonymous terms Third World or Two-Thirds World which can be seen as negative or

---

[2]The term "missionary" appears to have different connotations in North American and Latin American settings. For the former, "missionary" refers to "all sent to evangelize, plant churches or minister outside their homelands." For the latter, it is "all sent to evangelize, plant churches or minister cross-culturally whether in other lands or in their homelands" (Johnstone and Mandryk 2001, 757). In this study, however, the term "missionary" applies equally to Nationals who minister among their fellow countrymen, whether locally or cross-culturally.

patronizing and which are becoming obsolete since the collapse of the Communist Second World" (Johnstone and Mandryk 2001, 757).

Nouvelle Eglise Baptiste Missionnaire (NEBM): Synonymous with Haitian Missionary Church.

Pentecostals: "Those affiliated specifically to Pentecostal denominations committed to a Pentecostal theology usually including a post-conversion experience of a baptism in the Spirit, present exercise of the gifts of the Spirit and speaking in tongues" (Johnstone and Mandryk 2001, 757).

Vision: "A picture held in your mind's eye of the way things could or should be in the days ahead. Vision connotes a visual reality, a portrait of conditions that do not exist currently" (Barna 1992, 29).

Worldview: "The basic assumptions about reality which lie behind the beliefs and behavior of a culture" (Hiebert 2001, 45).

Statement of the Problem

As has been stated, the HMC initially lacked the outward focus necessary for missions. Based on interviews and data collected, I find this inward focus to be a fair representation of Haitian churches both in Haiti and overseas. I hypothesized that this limited vision stems from three probable sources:

(1)   Haitian natives and the missionaries generally consider Haiti a mission field, not a sending force.

(2)   Haitian believers in general have a confused understanding of the Great Commission.

(3)   The Haitian National Church has assumed it could not get involved in overseas missions because of its poverty level.

Early Response to the Study

Contrary to studies that focus on the progress of Protestantism, this research was intended to give an insider's "emic" (Hiebert 2001, 94) perspective on both the source of the problem and possible solutions to the restricted vision of the Haitian Church. Likewise, I aimed at expanding that vision into active involvement in cross-cultural missions among Haitian churches through preaching, teaching, seminars, missions conferences, workshops, and other overt measures.

Similarly, this study was designed to motivate National leaders and to mobilize churches to participate in the fulfillment of the Great Commission at a worldwide level. Some pastors in North America (New York, Florida, Boston, Chicago, and Canada) have already shown an interest in having the results of this research presented in their churches. One pastor e-mailed the author:

> Please reserve me a copy of your thesis, and of course I would like for you to come and give a presentation in my church whenever you come to visit the New York area.

Likewise, numerous churches in Haiti have already demonstrated the same enthusiasm to have a presentation of this study. One National missionary e-mailed the author:

> I have not seen or heard anyone who has dealt with this subject before . . . This theme will be without any shadow of a doubt a way for some to reflect and start over on solid ground.

I have also received an invitation to share the results of this research in a forum for key Haitian leaders in Florida in November 2003. Moreover, some local missions in Haiti as well as Bible schools are looking forward to the outcome of this research to possibly use it in their curriculum and leadership training. Similarly, laypeople, Bible schools, seminaries, students, as well as current and former missionaries, have already requested copies of this research for consultative purposes. Another Haitian missionary e-mailed me regarding this research:

> I believe that this thesis is a tremendous step in the right direction to discover a disease that has plagued the Haitian church at its core since its beginning. In order to provide the necessary cure for any kind of sickness, it is absolutely necessary to discover what causes it in the first place. Now with this thesis, we are about to unearth the root problem.

Several foreign missions agencies have manifested the desire to use this research for exploration upon its completion. In addition, a Chinese congregation has invited me to make a presentation at their church, and a well-respected magazine has also requested the submission of a summary article upon completion. The interest exhibited by the above was indicative of the importance of this subject and the need to explore it. As the Haitian Church was prepared to gather for an assessment of their 200 years of history, this research has become more influential for the vital missions aspect of the church. Finally, instead of making missions an abstract concept, unintentional, or merely one among many priorities of the church, this study reasserts the Great Commission as the main priority of the church according to Jesus' perspective.

Overall Objective of the Study

The research intention was to uncover factors of history, sociology, cultural anthropology, missiology, theology, religion, and missionary inspirations that may explain the limited vision of the Great Commission in the Haitian Church. Based on the data collected and interpreted, I was able to recommend a remedial plan that can help communicate that global vision.

Secondary Objectives of the Study

On a secondary level, the purpose was to encourage others to catch the vision of the Great Commission and to respond to it. In particular, the outcome of this research was to help the churches in Haiti and abroad shift their focus to a universal view of the missionary mandate. Likewise, it was hoped that local churches of other cultural identities could use the study comparatively for the purpose of strengthening their commitment to the Great Commission. Permission has been granted by the Moody Graduate School to translate this research into French and Creole for the benefit of Haitian leaders, Bible school and seminary students, and lay people.

Basic Assumptions of the Study

While making assumptions in this study, I was faced with the reality that one's own assessments can sometimes be overestimated. Out of a desire to protect my own integrity and that of the church under my care, I desired to find a way to ensure that my findings would be valid. I considered, for instance, that when members of a congregation responded to a pastor (researcher) that they might have in mind representing their own organization in a positive light. Others in ministry might raise the questions: "How fair would this researcher be?" and "How will these data be used?" This was not to say that participants were viewed as untruthful. Instead, it was to be expected for understandable reasons that complete objectivity could not be attained.

Because of the limitations of qualitative research of this nature, the questions to be presented on the questionnaire were prepared carefully, to restrict this bias as much as possible (see questionnaire in English and French in appendices 25 and 26, respectively). Out of 115 surveys given to potentially qualified respondents, 109 were returned completed. Apart from the survey questions, it became necessary to complement the overall data collection by using interviews and other types of communication. Respondents from among Evangelical and Pentecostal/Charismatic pastors and missions in Haiti and abroad were selected according to their availability.

Because of the cultural composition of the HMC, it was preferable to use two languages in the questionnaire (French and English) instead of three (if Creole were added). This decision was made due to the fact that even though Creole was spoken in general, yet many have difficulty reading it, and this could lead to misunderstandings. Therefore, regarding the questionnaire, it was assumed that:

(1) Those who filled out the questionnaire were representative of the larger population.

(2) Those who were illiterate disqualified themselves from filling out the questionnaire.

(3) Sufficient information was provided to enable participants to complete the questionnaire.

(4) Regardless of the language used, some participants might not be able to fully understand the issue at hand.

(5) Some people might feel intimidated by the questionnaire because they have never before filled out questionnaires in a church setting.

(6) The younger generation might have a better understanding of the missionary mandate and related factors, having evolved in a different context compared to previous generations.

(7) Haiti was still considered a mission field.

(8) Haitian believers in general had a limited view of the Great Commission.

(9) Having lived in the native culture; the Haitian believer can provide an insider's or "emic" perspective and firsthand knowledge.

(10) Missions is a confusing concept for the Haitian believers in general.

(11) Missions is often understood as limited to hospital visitation, helping the poor, and visiting prisoners in jail.

(12) The Haitian Church has an internal focus.

(13) There was a lack of adequate contextualization in the communication process of the gospel to the Haitian church in Haiti.

(14) The Great Commission has not been transmitted with a universal perspective in the Haitian Church.

(15) The National Church has assumed it cannot get involved in overseas missions because of its poverty level.

Finally, it is assumed that the limited vision of the Great Commission in the Haitian Church in Haiti and overseas can be singled out and remedied, and that to a certain extent, it was God's intention for *every* ethnic group (Haitians included) to go to the farthest parts of the earth (Matthew 28:18-20; Mark 16:15-16; Luke 24:46-48; John 20:21; Acts 1:8) with the gospel message. As this instruction has been given us by the Lord and Savior Jesus Christ, an underlying assumption is that the Great Commission must be achievable.

Limitations of the Study

The investigation of an issue such as a limited vision of the Great Commission in the Haitian Church as compared to other minority groups of people was a challenge. The author recognized some restrictions in terms of the scope of the research. Several local and foreign missions, missionaries, churches, as well as Haitian pastors of other denominations in Haiti and abroad, were not represented in this work due to inaccessibility of data. I selected the New Missionary Baptist Church (NMBC), where I serve as pastor, as a case study. I intended to apply the recommendations of this research primarily to the NMBC. Nonetheless, the research and conclusions can be customized or contextualized in other churches dealing with the same issues.

As there is undoubtedly additional information beyond the scope of this study that was related to a project of such magnitude, this research can only be seen as an incomplete attempt to deal with this subject matter.

This study was conducted at the HMC[3] in Evanston, Illinois. The average attendance is 65 people. In addition, other Evangelical and Pentecostal/Charismatic churches in Chicago were invited to participate. A questionnaire was designed, developed, and administered purposely to assess the cognitive, affective, and behavioral attitude of the participants. The accuracy of the pre-test and the test was contingent on the honesty of those who participated. It remained premature to assess the long-term effectiveness of this study. Nevertheless, the pastor or church leaders had the responsibility of implementing the results of this study.

Outline of the Study

Chapter 2 is a review of pertinent information about the literature associated with the Haitian Church. It encompassed aspects of historical and cultural perspectives, Evangelical and Pentecostal/Charismatic missions, and Haitian missions. This analysis was complemented with interviews and communication with National Church pastors, missionaries, missions leaders and agencies, Bible seminary presidents, students, and laypeople as well as related studies to determine which factors have contributed to the restrictive view of the missionary mandate in the Haitian Church.

---

[3] HMC was later renamed New Missionary Baptist Church (NMBC) to emphasize its new focus on global missions.

Chapter 3 presents a description of the ministry setting. Also included is discussion of the subjects and population, the sample selection, the survey instrument (questionnaire), the procedures, and the type of analysis as well as how the data were collected, organized, and analyzed. The purpose of my analysis was to determine whether or not the Haitian believers had a geographically limited vision of the Great Commission and to discover if there may be a difference in understanding between male and female, youth and adults.

Chapter 4 covers the collection, analysis, and interpretation of the data from congregants to assess what they were thinking about the Great Commission.

Chapter 5 is a summary of the study, followed by my conclusions and recommendations. Following chapter 5 are the bibliography and 28 appendices. The appendices are listed by title in the table of contents. The materials in the appendices include definitions of culture, demographics on missions related to Haiti, a list of interviewees for this study, English and French copies of the questionnaire used to gather research data as well as a summary of the data collected, a full range of helps for promoting missions in local churches, a brief outline of VIGCOM (a ministry dedicated to helping ordinary people make a greater contribution to fulfilling the Great Commission), and a list of abbreviations used in this book.

CHAPTER 1:
THEOLOGICAL AND BIBLICAL BASIS
OF THE STUDY

It is commonly assumed that Scriptures bear witness to the fact that "God is a missionary God". This section is an overview of some facts about God's purpose regarding missionary activities. A brief consideration of some Old Testament texts reveals that few can argue that God is other than a God of purpose in relation to missions (cf. Psalms 19; 33:4-6; 139). When He created the universe, God demonstrated His ingenious power and majesty and said, "It is good" (Genesis 1:4, 10, 12, 18, 21, 25, 31).

Although the Bible emphasizes the transcendence of God, it also teaches that God is the God of relationships. Men and women were created in the image and likeness of God (Genesis 1:26-27) as relational, rational, moral, and spiritual beings. As "the seminal head" of the human race, Adam's disobedience brought death and universal condemnation to the entire race. The apostle Paul made this clear in Romans chapter 5: "There is universal sinfulness, guilt, condemnation and death in and through Adam (Romans 5:12).

As revealed in Scriptures, God's intention from eternity past was to save mankind. The Old Testament abounds in examples of the universality of God's missionary intent. For instance, Genesis 12:1 was the call of Abram to be a blessing to the nations of the world. The book of Jonas deals with a rebel prophet who ran in the opposite direction instead of seeing his enemies being spared from destruction. These were some illustrations in the Old Testament. Nonetheless, it was beyond the scope of this section to enumerate all of them. Other scholars such as Winter and Hawthorne (1999); Verkuyl (1978); Kane (1976); Stott (1975); Peters (1972); Lindsell (1966); Vicedom (1965); Glover (1964); Anderson (1961); and Carver (1951) to name a few scholars on the subject, have dealt with this theme in detail. Yahweh is the Sovereign of all nations. In His divine purpose, He chose Israel as the channel through

17

which the Messianic King would come to rule over all creation (Genesis 49:10).

In the Gospels, Jesus gave the command to bring the universal message to the nations following His death and resurrection (Matthew 28:18-20, Mark 15-16). The Book of Acts and the Epistles revealed the application of the Great Commission to the needs of fallen man (Acts 13; 15-28). In Revelation, the final achievement of God's missionary vision was realized with the gathering of a great multitude from all nations and kingdoms to worship Him (Revelation 7:9-12).

The next section zeroes in on study of the Great Commission through the eyes of each of the four evangelists (Matthew, Mark, Luke, and John). The texts are quoted from the New International Version (NIV) of 1995. Each Gospel is studied separately. However, the Gospel of Luke and the Book of Acts are examined together. I concluded with a composite perspective of the missionary mandate, presented according to Jesus' model.

The Missionary Mandate in the Gospel of MATTHEW

Then Jesus came to them and said, All authority in heaven and on earth has been given to me. Therefore go and make disciples of all nations, baptizing them in the name of the Father and of the Son and of the Holy Spirit, and teaching them to obey everything I have commanded you. And surely I am with you always, to the very end of the age. (Matthew 28:18-20)

In the final verses of his Gospel, Matthew encapsulated his perspectives on what Jesus started to do from the beginning. This final passage appears to be the key to unlocking the overall purpose of the book. The Great Commission as located in Matthew 28:18-20 was not randomly placed, considering the strategic position it occupies in the Gospel (Wilkins 1992, 186).

The writer of the Gospel carefully selected and arranged his material to link the epilogue (Matthew 28:18-20) with the prologue (chapters 1-2) in light of Jesus' role as the Sovereign Lord of all peoples (France 1985, 411). For instance, one of Matthew's concerns in the opening verses was to inform his readers about Jesus' mission. He presented three facts in the genealogy of Jesus that were worth considering.

First, Jesus is the son of David (1:1). This recurring theme (1:1; 9:27; 12:23; 15:22; 20:30,31; 21:9,15; 22:42) as expressed by a variety of people (the blind, the crowd, Gentiles, children, and Jesus) pointed to Christ as the fulfillment of God's promise to David. Though Jesus came from the Davidic lineage as the promised Jewish Messiah, Matthew demonstrated that He is the Messiah of all peoples *"both Jews and Gentiles"* (8:5-13; 15:21-28).

Secondly, Jesus is the son of Abraham (1:1). This reference to Jesus in the introductory verse (1:1) showed that the blessings promised through Abraham's offspring to all nations (Genesis 22:18) found fulfillment in Jesus the Messiah. Though Matthew presented Jesus as a genuine Jew, he wanted to prepare his audience from the beginning (1:1) for the commission to make disciples of all peoples (28:18-20). Both texts (Genesis 22:18 and Matthew 28:19) used the same expression, "all nations." As a result, Jesus is presented as the fulfillment of the kingdom promised to David and the blessings promised to Gentiles through Abraham (Gaebelein 1984, 62).

Thirdly, the names of four Gentile women (Tamar, Rahab, Ruth, and Bathsheba) were intentional (Matt 1:3, 5, 6). Unlike the wives of the Patriarchs, Matthew purposefully chose these women as a hint foretelling God's intention to include the Gentiles in His plan (28:19) (Keener 1997, 54-55).

Furthermore, Matthew's concluding statement of Jesus' promise in the Great Commission, "I am with you always" (28:20) is reminiscent of "Immanuel" (1:23), which means "God with us" (France 1985, 80).

Jesus' association with the Gentiles was a recurrent motif in Matthew (2:1-12; 4:12-17; 8:5-13; 15:21-28). His inaugural preaching ministry (4:12-17) in "Galilee of the Gentiles" emerged as a fulfillment of prophesy that anticipated the commission to go to all nations (28:19). Moreover, the setting of the eschatological discourse indicated Matthew's concern for the Gentile mission (24:14). The fact that Jesus visited several regions inhabited by Gentiles during His earthly ministry (4:13) suggested that He had a worldwide mission in view (4:25; 8:28; 16:13; 28:18-20). All the above references seemed to point out that the Gentiles obtained adequate access to Jesus compared to that afforded to the Jews.

Matthew did not wait until the end to show how Jesus paved the way to reach the nations. To the contrary, he displayed at least five crucial steps leading to that point.

The first step was the *calling* of the disciples. Jesus summoned His disciples to bond with Him in the work of disciple-making: "Come follow me…and I will make you fishers of men" (4:19).

The second step was *teaching*. He taught them extensively about the things pertaining to the kingdom and the end times (chapters 5-7; 13; 18; 24-25). Though there was a cost to follow Him (8:18-22; 16:24-28), nonetheless, Jesus showed the disciples the great need for the harvest (9:35-38).

The third step was *choosing*. As the disciples prayed for the harvest, Jesus chose twelve men in whom He would invest His time (Matthew 10:1-4).

The fourth step was *training*. Jesus first commissioned them to go to the "lost sheep of Israel to preach the message of the kingdom, to heal the sick, to raise the dead, to make clean those who had leprosy and drive out demons" (10:5-10). He trained the disciples as they learned among their own people, prior to sending them to other nations.

Therefore, the missionary training of the disciples was foundational to the fifth step, which culminated in His *sending* them on the universal mission of the Great Commission (28:18-20).

In summary, Matthew's universal commission could not be elsewhere than in its strategic position. Even though Jesus' disciples were given hints as to the universality of His mission, they were not equipped to be sent at the beginning of their ministry. They needed to be taught, chosen, and trained before carrying out the mandate to disciple the nations. The vision imparted in Galilee (4:19) and the mission yet to be fulfilled had found their expression in the Great Commission (28:19). Therefore, disciple-making was the main emphasis in Matthew's Gospel.

The Missionary Mandate in the Gospel of MARK

He said to them, Go into all the world and preach the good news to all creation. Whoever believes and is baptized will be saved, but whoever does not believe will be condemned. (Mark 16:15-16)

Jesus' final message to His disciples as reported in Mark 16:15 was the ultimate commission to preach the Good News to all creation. Mark portrayed Jesus' vision from the beginning as evangelistic (1:1). No task was more important to Him according to Mark than to begin His ministry by preaching the Good News (1:14) and preparing His followers to reach the world (1:17). However, the announcement of the Good News in (1:1) was both intentional and significant. It was intentional because from Mark's perspective, the Good News (1:1) revolved about the person of Jesus Christ (Cole 1993, 104).

Mark presented Jesus as the proclaimer of God's kingdom, preaching the Good News and calling people to repentance and belief (1:15). Since Mark probably targeted a Gentile audience, Jesus' preaching appeared to extend to that community as well (3:8; 5:1; 6:56; 7:24,31). Furthermore, Jesus anticipated that the time would come for His gospel to be preached to all nations (13:10), throughout the world (14:9), and to all creation (16:15). Those "who believe and are baptized will be saved" (16:16), but the rejection of the gospel was equivalent to self-condemnation (9:37) (Cole 1993, 71).

Jesus always believed that His followers would be the ones to bring the gospel to all creation. Mark did not remain silent about

21

that. He laid out five vital steps demonstrating Jesus' vision to reach all creation.

The first step was the *calling* of Jesus' followers. Jesus went alongside the Sea of Galilee to call ordinary men who were willing to learn, to be molded and to be used by God. "Come, follow me," Jesus said, "and I will make you fishers of men" (1:16-20).

The second step was *teaching*. The disciples were taught about the kingdom of God (1:21; 2:13; 4:1,34). Early in His ministry, Jesus exposed His followers to various situations that were designed to teach them (1:21-28, 32-39; 2:12, 15-17, 23-28; 3:1-6, 7-12; 4:1-34; 6:30-52; 8:1-21).

The third step was *choosing*. He went to the mountain to choose and appoint those He would send out to preach (3:13-19).

Besides teaching, Jesus was also *training* the disciples. That was the fourth step. He spent a great deal of time training His disciples for the work of the ministry of the gospel (1:23, 29, 32, 36, 40; 2:3, 3:1-6, 7-12). Very early in the training sessions, Jesus began to instill in His disciples a sense of responsibility (to reach out to others). For that reason, He gave them evangelistic assignments (3:9; 6:7). Invested with the same authority as their Master, they preached repentance, cast out demons, anointed sick people with oil and healed them (6:7-13).

These evangelistic activities provided the groundwork for the fifth step, which was the *sending* out for the universal mission of the Great Commission (16:15-16).

According to Mark, the Messiah is the Son of God. His missionary purpose was to show that Jesus came to give His life for sinners (2:17; 15:39). In this context, the events and teaching that led up to His crucifixion were deliberate (10:45). The cross represented the price of preaching the gospel (15:29-32). Those who followed Jesus were not treated differently; instead, they had the same work to do (10:39). From that point of view, Mark's vision of the Messiah conflicted with the expectations of the disciples (9:10, 32), who anticipated a conquering warrior. Instead, by following their Lord, the disciples had the same responsibility to proclaim the Good News beyond their own ethnic group (1:38-39; 3:7-12; 7:24-30; 13:10; 16:15).

In summary, the universal commission (16:15) recorded by Mark is presented as part of Jesus' purpose from the beginning (1:1, 14). However, because His vision was to reach the whole creation, Jesus needed time to call, teach, recruit, train, and prepare His disciples for the task ahead of them. The vision announced in Galilee (1:17) was fully presented throughout Mark's account of Jesus' ministry and more so after Jesus' resurrection (16:15). Mark highlighted the evangelistic component of Jesus' teaching: the preaching of the Good News to all creation. From beginning to end, Mark's perspective of Jesus ministry was evangelistic (1:1; 16:15).

The Missionary Mandate in the Gospel of LUKE and the Book of ACTS

He told them, this is what is written: The Christ will suffer and rise from the dead on the third day, and repentance and forgiveness of sins will be preached in His name to all nations, beginning at Jerusalem. You are witnesses of these things." (Luke 24:46-48)

But you will receive power when the Holy Spirit comes on you; and you will be my witnesses in Jerusalem, and in all Judea and Samaria, and to the ends of the earth. (Acts 1:8)

Since the Gospel of Luke is a companion volume of the Book of Acts (Luke 1:1-4; Acts 1:1-2), I treated them collectively.

It would be difficult to believe that Luke did not write his Gospel and the Book of Acts with a missionary purpose in mind (Luke 1:1; Acts 1:1, 8; 8:5; 28:16). In fact, the Great Commission as given in both texts (Luke 24:47 and Acts 1:8) demonstrates that Jesus wanted to focus on the preaching of the gospel to all nations. Likewise, the universal message of Jesus Christ was designed for all people "Luke 2:1, 3:4-6; Acts 2:17" (Guthrie 1990, 102).

Though the Good News was introduced in the presence of high political figures (Luke 2:1-3; 3:1-2), the message of salvation was intended for all strata of society (Luke 1:52-55; 2:8; 4:26; 5:27-32; 7:1-6; 14:13, 18:3). For this reason, Jesus was called the friend of sinners (7:34; 15:2). Likewise, the record of Acts demonstrated that the gospel penetrated all echelons of society (10:1; 26:20) until it reached the Roman Empire in Paul's days (Acts 28:31) through obedience to the Great Commission mandate (1:8).

From the beginning, one of Luke's emphases was to present the gospel of salvation for mankind (Luke 3:6). Although this message was encapsulated in the suffering, death, and resurrection of Jesus Christ (Luke 24:46), man had the responsibility for personal appropriation of salvation through repentance (Luke 24:47). Jesus preached this message everywhere (Luke 4:43). The disciples did the same in the life of the early church (Acts 8:4, 12, 25; 10:42; 14:7). In fact, because of the lostness of mankind, Jesus was sent for that redemptive purpose (Luke 4:43; 5:32; 19:10) for which He was willing to die (Luke 9:22, 44; 18:32). The essence of His message was to call sinners to repentance, which was a key term in Luke (13:3-5; 15:7; 18:9-14; 19:7-9; 24:47). The Book of Acts reinforced the same message (2:38; 3:19; 5:31; 8:22), and everywhere people were called to do the same (17:30). Even King Agripa was no exception (26:20) (Bloomberg 1997, 142).

From Luke's perspective, the gospel moved in geographical sequence. Jesus led His mission to Gentile territories of Samaria (9:51-62; 17:11) and Perea (13:22-19:27) and to Jerusalem (19:28-44). The early disciples picked up the gospel at Jerusalem and carried it throughout the known world (Acts 28:31).

In order for the message to infiltrate the world of that day, Luke demonstrated the steps Jesus took to prepare His disciples for that task. At least five steps stand out.

Again, the first step was the *calling* of the disciples. After a miraculous fishing event at the lake of Gennesareth, Jesus called His followers: "and so were James and John, the sons of Zebedee, Simon's partners." Then Jesus said to Simon, "Don't be afraid; from now on you will catch men." So they pulled their boats up on shore, left everything and followed Him (Luke 5:10-11).

The second step was *teaching*. The disciples were taught the things of the kingdom of God (Luke 6:17-49; 8:10).

The third step was *choosing*. Among the evangelists, only Luke emphasized the significance of prayer in Jesus' choice of His disciples. They were chosen (Luke 6:12-16; Acts 1:24-26) to further the work that was committed to their care (Luke 24:47).

The fourth step was *training*. Luke mentioned that the disciples were sent out twice (Luke 9:2, 6; 10:1). Thus they were given training to preach the kingdom of God, to heal the sick, to drive out all demons, and to cure the sick with God's power and authority.

Sending was the final step in their preparation to preach to all nations. Equally in his Gospel and in the Book of Acts, Luke portrayed how the disciples carried out the missionary mandate entrusted to them, culminating in Paul's final years in Rome (Acts 28:31) boldly preaching the kingdom of God and teaching about the Lord Jesus Christ to all who came to Him.

In summary, Luke presented in his two volumes (Luke and Acts) a missionary Gospel. Jesus' missionary vision according to Luke was fulfilled in the life of His disciples. Luke emphasized the proclamation of the universal message of salvation through the finished work of Christ. Through the power of the Holy Spirit, Jesus' missionary vision was fulfilled in the life of His disciples. The message was boldly proclaimed, and salvation was assured to those who repent of their sins.

The Missionary Mandate in the Gospel of JOHN

Again Jesus said, "Peace be with you! As the Father has sent me, I am sending you." (John 20:21)

The Great Commission as recorded by John was reminiscent of one of the overall themes of the book -- Jesus as sent on a mission by the Father (20:16; 5:23; 6:38; 12:49). From this writer's perspective, Jesus came with the clear mission to save the world

(3:17). The world recognized Him to be the Savior of the world (4:42). The world into which He came had no life (6:33). In a world filled with darkness and sin, Jesus was the only One who could bring light to the world (1:9) and take away its sin (1:29). John presented Jesus as the Messiah (1:41; 4:25), the Eternal Son of God (17:3; 6:27). He is the Life-Saver (5:21; 10:28), the One in Whom one must believe in order to have eternal life (20:31, 3:15, 16). The whole purpose of John's Gospel was to proclaim that only belief in Jesus can guarantee eternal life. To support this claim, John intentionally described the seven miracles in his Gospel account (2:11; 4:43-54; 5:1-15; 6:1-14, 16-24; 9:1-12, and 11:38-44) (Morris 1992, 684).

Another aspect of Jesus' mission according to John was to prepare His disciples to continue His work. He supplied the identity of the Son of God in the seven "I am" statements of John 6:35, 8:12; 10:7; 10:11; 11:25; 14:6, and 15:5. John did not wait until the end of his Gospel to show how Jesus equipped His disciples for world evangelism. He presented the five steps Jesus followed to prepare His disciples.

The first step was *calling* them to follow Him (John 1:35-51). Jesus replied to two of John's disciples, "Come and you will see" (1:39). To Philip Jesus said, "Follow me" (1:43).

The second step was *teaching*. Jesus taught His disciples under different circumstances (2:1-11, 13-22; 6:1-15, 22-59; 10:1-21). Most importantly, He taught them extensively about His dependence on the Father for the mission He was sent to accomplish (4:34-38; 5:17-47; 6:35-52; 8:16-54; 10:15-38; 12:44-50; 14:2-31; 17:1-25). If the disciples were to take Jesus' mission into the world, they would need to be dependent on the Father who would send the Spirit to teach them all things (14:25-26). The disciples' call to missions was not only oriented around the person of Jesus Christ and His work, but equally around God Himself.

The third step was *choosing* the twelve. Even though John did not focus on the time (when) and place (where) the disciples were chosen, he stated clearly that Jesus chose the twelve (6:70; 13:18; 15:16, 19).

The fourth step was *training* the disciples. They were trained (3:22-36) and challenged in a different cultural setting not to postpone the harvest (4:36).

The fifth step involved *sending* the disciples into the world. The Father sent the Son Who in return sent His disciples with the duty to gather His flock around the world into God's family (10:16; 17:1-26; 20:21). Prior to sending the disciples on missions, Jesus was destined to the cross, not only to die for the whole nation of Israel (11:51), but for the world as well (1:29) (Morris 1992, 273, 350, 436, 509, 550, 623, 743).

In summary, the commission given by the Lord Jesus Christ in John 20:21 was an outgrowth of Jesus' intention from the beginning (1:29). Jesus' disciples were given hints as to the worldwide feature of His missions (1:29; 3:16-19; 4:42; 6:14-51; 8:12-26; 10:36; 11:27; 12:19-47), yet they were not equipped to be sent at the beginning of their ministry. *Needless to say, it was a prerequisite for them to be called, taught, chosen, and trained before they were sent to carry out the mandate of the Great Commission.* Therefore, John highlighted the global evangelistic aspect of the missionary mandate (20:21).

COMPOSITE Perspective of the Missionary Mandate

Four different presentations of the Great Commission were examined through the eyes of the Gospel writers. Each author phrased Jesus' missionary mandate in his own unique way. Matthew emphasized the discipleship of all nations (Matthew 28:18-20). Mark on the other hand highlighted the evangelism of all creation (Mark. 16:15-16). From a geographical standpoint, Luke emphasized the evangelism of all nations starting from Jerusalem and, in the power of the Holy Spirit, reaching the ends of the earth (Luke 24:47-28; Acts 28:31). Finally, John accentuated a worldwide evangelistic effort with a striking parallelism of the Father commissioning the Son and the Son commissioning the disciples (John 20:21).

27

Since each Gospel writer presented Jesus' Great Commission in a different way, one might think that favoring one over another might lead to certain methodological problems, both in teaching and practice. To the contrary, Luke's perspective to reach the nations was to start at "Jerusalem" (locally) while ministering (cross-culturally) "to the ends of the earth". If Mark 16:15-16 or John 20:21 were favored as the most important version of the Great Commission, the predisposition might be to evangelize everywhere (cross-culturally) while neglecting "Jerusalem" (local -- Luke's prominent focus) or overlooking "disciple-making" (Matthew's emphasis). Mark and John were not preoccupied either with the location of departure or with making disciples. Finally, if Matthew was chosen as the dominant version of the Great Commission, the inclination might be to overemphasize disciple-making at the expense of the other facets of the Great Commission.

The fact of the matter is that Matthew, Mark, and John focus respectively on disciple-making and the evangelization of all creation and of the world without any specific reference to geography. On the other hand, the Gospel of Luke and the Book of Acts point to "Jerusalem" as the point of departure to evangelize the nations and the ends of the earth. Each version of the missionary mandate taken separately appears to show both strengths and weaknesses. Therefore, it is suggested that the Great Commission was modeled after Jesus' global vision, which put identical emphasis on disciple-making as well as on evangelism and equally on geographical structure.

Jesus gave one Great Commission with five different emphases (Matthew, Mark, Luke, John, and Acts) to His Church. Instead of choosing one emphasis over another, it is important for the Church to appreciate the different aspects of the Great Commission as taught by the Lord Jesus Christ. The Great Commission started with evangelism, continued with conversion and repentance followed by identification with the death and resurrection of Jesus Christ (which symbolized the entrance of the believer into the community of faith), and ended with making disciples.

As presented by the four writers, the Great Commission embodies an overall outline of the missionary assignment given by

Jesus to His Church. From a grammatical perspective, two imperatives were found in the missionary mandate, together with three participles and the geographical note (Matthew 28:18-20; Mark 16:15-16, Luke 24:46-48, Acts 1:8). The commands were to "make disciples" and "preach the gospel" complemented by "going," "baptizing," and "teaching," and followed by the geographical notes. The imperatives were fundamental and articulated the heart of the commission, while the participles symbolized the ways in which the task could be accomplished.

It must be kept in mind that the Great Commission did not set forth all the responsibilities of the Church in this world or the whole mission of the Church. Its purpose was to focus the Church on reaching out to the lost and unchurched people of the world without distinction of their race, color, ethnic group, or religion.

It can be surmised that the Great Commission was part of a deliberate plan from eternity past to bring the nations of the earth to God Himself (Revelation 7:9-12). The Great Commission was the focal point of God's agenda to reach the nations of the world. As such, it was a mandate calling all of Jesus' disciples to evangelize the world and to make disciples of all nations without exception. The whole world must be reached with the message of the salvation of God in Christ Jesus. Since Jesus gave such directive to His Church, it must be possible to fulfill it.

RIPE NOW!

CHAPTER 2:
REVIEW OF LITERATURE

Studying the Issues

A national survey conducted by Barna Research in 1994 reported that "9 out of 10 American adults (86%) cannot accurately define the meaning of the "Great Commission." The same survey concluded that "only 4% of adults could define the 'Great Commission,' quote John 3:16, and define 'the gospel.'"[4]

Anyone with a basic knowledge of the missionary mandate might think that Christ's command has been received without "confusion." But that is simply an assumption -- not necessarily the reality. In fact, David Hesselgrave presented in *Evangelical Dictionary of World Missions* an historical overview of a wide variety of interpretations and applications of the Great Commission throughout 2000 years of history (Moreau 2000, 412-414). Furthermore, Robert Coleman in *The Great Commission Lifestyle* shared the view that many people are bewildered about the Great Commission (Coleman 1992, 12).

It is within this context of an historical overview of interpreting the Great Commission that I addressed the question: *What factors that can cause confusion about Christ's missionary mandate have specific ramifications within the Haitian Church?* I sought the answer to this question in my review of the literature associated with the Haitian church as well as in interviews, conversations, and communication with National Church pastors, missionaries, mission leaders and agencies, a Bible seminary president, students, and lay people.

Informants for the study were selected based on their availability. An open-ended format was used for the interviews. Thirty-three (33) people were either interviewed in person by phone or communicated with me face to face in Creole, French, or

---

[4]Source: http://www.barna.org /cgi-bin/PageCategory.asp?CategoryID=18).

31

English (see appendix 7): one (1) evangelist, eight (8) pastors in Haiti and abroad (Nationals and others), seventeen (17) missionaries (14 Haitians and 3 others), two (2) Presidents of a Christian University, two (2) former Presidents of indigenous para-church organizations, one (1) foreign agency (regional coordinator), one (1) former student of a seminary, and one (1) lay person.

In this chapter, aspects of the historical and cultural perspective of three particular groups were of interest: (1) Evangelical Missions, (2) Pentecostal/Charismatic Missions, and (3) Haitian Missions. These areas of interest were examined to find out what factors could help account for the restrictive view of the missionary mandate in the Haitian Church. Despite the general overview, it was beyond the scope of this work to make a comprehensive examination of all past missions work in Haiti, and apologies are extended to any involved in worthy efforts whose work has not been discussed in this book.

Background Information about Haiti

Haiti is situated less than 1,000 miles from the shores of Florida. A little bit smaller than the state of Maryland (in the USA), Haiti is located in the Caribbean between the North Atlantic Ocean and the Caribbean Sea, west of the Dominican Republic with which it shares a border. Although the native Arawaks named the land Haiti (Ayiti), Christopher Columbus in 1492 named it Hispaniola (Little Spain). The French, in 1697, called it Saint-Domingue (relating to French missionaries after the order of Saint Dominic). At Haiti's independence in 1804, Jean-Jacques Dessalines gave to the first Black independent nation in the world the Arawaks' name of Haiti.

The unique mix of religious beliefs and practices that now exists in Haiti reflects the indigenous Indians who occupied the land, the Africans who were brought to Haiti, and the Christian missions that have existed in Haiti since 1492.

FIG. 1. MAP OF HAITI

Source: *The World Factbook*, http://www.infoplease.com/ipa/A0748754.html

Fombrun in his History of Haiti (1986, 14, 18) suggests that the Indians who occupied the land worshipped many gods called "Zemes." Likewise, these native Haitians worshipped the moon, the sun, the thunderstorm, and some animals. They bore "amulets and charms," superstitious signs for self-protection. Their priests, called "butios," served as witchcraft doctors. People who hold such beliefs are commonly known to belong to an animistic religion coupled with a tribal worldview.

This way of perceiving reality (animism) is summarized under three headings by C. Gordon Olson in *What in the World Is God Doing?* (1993, 167-170): (1) Necrolatry, (2) Spirit Worship, and (3) Naturism.

Olson relates that in Necrolatry (worship of the dead), there is a sense of fear that the departed ancestor can harm the living person unless he/she is helped by some appropriate ceremonies.

Olson goes on to explain that in Spirit Worship, people believe in the existence of personal spirits or demons that inhabit the earth, air, fire, water, trees, and mountains as well as animal life. This type of Spirit Worship is commonly known as shamanism. Shamanism relies on a form of imitative magic seeking "to bring harm to an enemy by attacking a representation of him, such as a voodoo doll." Within the practice of Magic, "the blood of a predatory animal may be drunk to gain the strength of the animal. This custom goes further in cannibalism which is materialized by eating the enemy as a way to gain his power." Fetishism, according to Olson, involves the attributing of magical powers to objects and putting one's trust in such powers, and is also a part of the practice of Magic.

Olson describes Naturism as "the personification and worship of the forces of nature such as animals, stars, moon, sun..."

Olson relates that animistic religion and culture have the following pervading effects on their devotees:

(1) The whole life is pervaded with fear.

(2) The absence of love, consolation and hope is all-encompassing.

(3) There are no absolutes of morality. Sin is perceived as a violation of culture, custom, and natural forces.

(4) The lack of relationship with God causes a fatalistic attitude since all the events of life are predetermined and controlled by nature or demons.

For the purposes of this study, Voodoo is held as akin to Vodou, vaudou or vodun and refers to a worldview, a trait of the Haitian culture, and not the culture itself as some claimed it to be. Recently (April 4, 2003), Voodoo was promoted as an official religion in Haiti in which priests, witchcraft doctors (Boko) now have legal rights to perform baptismal, marriage, and funeral ceremonies. (World Evangelical Alliance. Accessed 27 September 2003[5].)

While much additional information is available on the history of religion in Haiti, it is not my primary intent in this book to review this body of work. Suffice it to say that one article by Charles Storch of the *Chicago Tribune* described the religious mix in Haiti as "a concoction brewed over centuries" by slaves from Africa (particularly the western areas now called Nigeria and Benin), who introduced Voodoo, and by Caribbean Indians and French colonialists, who added aspects of Roman Catholicism and the secret societies of Freemasonry (October 21, 1999, section 5, page 1, 13).

Van Rheenen provides the following description of Voodoo practices in Haiti:

> Voodoo of Haiti highlights spiritual metamorphosis; spirits are thought to change form. For example, human beings might take animal shapes and mingle with zombies and spirits....Voodoo ceremonies create an emotional environment in which spirit possession takes place. The practitioner enters a trance and serves as the chwal (horse) of the spirit...using that person's body and voice, the spirit sings, dances, and eats with the people and offers them advice and chastisement. The people, in turn, offer the spirit a wide variety of gifts and acts of obeisance whose

---

[5] Source: http://www.worldevangelical.org/persec_haiti_26aug03 .html.

goal is to placate the spirit and ensure his or her continuing protection. (1991, 26, 191)

Voodoo is pervasive in religious belief in Haitian religions, even within the Church. Vodouists believe in a distant supreme god, but trust more in a vast number of spirits to provide help, protection, and guidance. The spirits are said to demand ritual service and to communicate to followers by possessing them while they are in a trance state. In his book, *The Growing Church in Haiti*, Hammon Johnson noted:

Voodoo is a worldview held by the majority of Haitians. It suggests incantations, mysterious ceremonies, and maybe even human sacrifices. Voodoo is a type of worship carried over in essence from Africa. Haitians in general do not make distinctions between Roman Catholic and Voodoo practitioners as being two separate religious systems. The syncretism of African religious patterns with elements of Roman Catholic is thorough-going and pervasive. (1970, 16-19)

Historical and Cultural Perspective of Missions in Haiti

The historical and cultural setting of Christian missions in Haiti is divided into two segments: (1) Roman Catholic and (2) Evangelical and Pentecostal/Charismatic.

ROMAN CATHOLIC MISSIONS

The history of Christian missions in Haiti begins with the 1492 arrival of Christopher Columbus, who initiated the Roman Catholic religion with the cross of Christ and the conquering flag of Spain. However, upon their arrival, the "Spaniards" thrust aside the Indians' culture and forced Roman Catholic religion on the Arawak

36

Indians. Those who refused to embrace that creed were punished, even by death. Nonetheless, the "Spaniards" failed to eradicate Indian beliefs. Hence, this blend created a syncretism appearing as a layer of Roman Catholic belief superimposed upon Indian popular beliefs. As a result, a new religion emerged in the new world with the older gods supplanted by Roman Catholic saints.

Due to forced labor and other factors, the autochthonous polytheist population of the Arawak Indians diminished markedly. This led to the importation of African slaves to supersede the Arawak Indians. As they arrived in the colony, the Africans added a different cultural component to the preexisting religious mix of the new world. The French took over the colony through the treaty of Ryswick in 1697; and with the intensification of African slave importation into the colony, the number of Africans reached 450,000, or 90 percent of the existing population by 1789 (Leyburn 1941, 18).

During this period of Haiti's history, priests and missionaries forced African slaves to be baptized in order to become Roman Catholic (Jeanty 1990, 46). As a result, a syncretism developed between the vestiges of Indian beliefs, African myth and ritual, and Roman Catholicism. Later, the influence of Voodoo increased when the Vatican and France broke off ties with Haiti following its independence in 1804. Relating to that period, Leyburn commented:

> The longer the schism endured, the farther [sic] the people grew away from the doctrines and practices of a religion in which they had never been fully grounded....Religion existed during those years, but it was a strange gallimaufry of Catholicism and folk belief. (Leyburn 1966, 119-120)

The Vatican resumed mission activities in Haiti by the Concordat of 1860; and as a result, Roman Catholicism then became the state religion in the country for more than a century. Nonetheless, it was already too late to reverse the damage of Voodoo influence mixed with Roman Catholic belief. In that context, Heneise said:

Roman Catholicism was almost forgotten as the Virgin Mary became the goddess *Erzulie*...and St. Anthony as *Papa Legba,* the keeper of the door. Thus these and hundreds of other African spirit-gods became associated with the names and images of saints of the Roman Catholic Church. (Heneise 1999, 9)

In summary, just as the Spanish had disregarded the culture and worldview of the Indians in imposing the Roman Catholic religion, the French missionaries assumed the same disregard towards the African slaves. Both approaches led to syncretism because the core of the recipient culture was not influenced. In such an animistic context, embedded in a Voodoo worldview, Evangelical and Pentecostal/Charismatic missionaries faced a complicated task at the dawn of their missions in Haiti. These Protestant missionaries would need a different approach than their predecessors had used in order to succeed in planting and reproducing churches that would reach the world for Christ. With this confusing and pseudo-Christian background dominating the socio-cultural context that existed by 1816, the history of Evangelical and Pentecostal/Charismatic missions in Haiti began.

EVANGELICAL AND PENTECOSTAL/CHARISMATIC MISSIONS

The history of Evangelical and Pentecostal/Charismatic missions in Haiti is the focus of this study. A twofold subdivision is suggested: (1) The Exploration Phase, 1816-1916 and (2) the Extension Phase, 1917 – Present.

The Exploration Phase, 1816-1916

Though some have argued in favor of 1807 as the date when Evangelical missions history began in Haiti (Barrett, Kurian, and Johnson 2001, 340), others have maintained the later date of 1816 (Heneise 1999, 14; Jeanty 1990, 57; Romain 1986, 47). Among the denominations represented during the first period were: Methodist (1817), Episcopal (1823), Baptist (1823) and Seventh-Day Adventist (1879), all from England, the United States, and Jamaica. These missionaries responded to the need to bring the gospel to the Haitians, even at the cost of their own lives. By 1823, there were already many Afro-Americans spreading the gospel in some major cities in the country. By the next decade, the first Haitian church was planted by Afro-American missionaries. Statistics in 1842 showed 1,200 converts in Haiti (Romain 1986, 55, 93).

It should be noted that these missions represented a number of different organizations. For instance, Dr. Charles-Poisset Romain discussed six different groups of Baptist affiliation connected to this early period: (1) Baptists from America (1823); (2) Baptist Missionary Society from England (1845); (3) Abolitionist Baptists (1845); (4) Independent Baptists (1880); (5) Baptists from Jamaica (1885); (6) and more recently, Baptists from America (1923). (Romain 1986, 57). (See appendix 5 for more detail.)

Likewise, the Afro-American missions to Haiti came from varied sources. The American Episcopal Mission alone sent 110 black missionaries. The following organizations sent missionaries of "color" to Haiti: Baptist Missionary Society of Massachusetts, Baptist General Convention, American Baptist Free Mission Society, Independent American Negro, Independent Baptist Immigrants, American Abolitionists, British Baptists, American Negro Missionary to Canada, Baptist Missionary Society of London, Jamaican Baptist Missionary Society, Independent Baptist, Baptist Missionary Society of Jamaica, Lott Carey Convention of Negro Baptists. (González 2001, 319-320); Heneise 1999, 35, 63, 79, 81; Casséus 1997, 171-172; Romain 1986, 55, 57)

Among the pioneers were many visiting missionaries who explored the milieu while winning souls for Christ. Although some wanted to prolong their stay, inadequate funds, illnesses, persecutions, political instability, death, and other factors brought their mission to an end. When their missions ended, their work disappeared, leaving abandoned congregations "destitute of leadership." By the end of the first century missions of Evangelicals in the country (1816-1916), many churches were launched in different parts of the country; and Evangelicals were about 0.6 percent of the total population of 2,124,000 Haitians by 1920 (Romain 1986, 90, 102). The remaining population practiced Roman Catholicism associated with Voodoo. Therefore, long roads were yet to be traveled before the gospel would reach all Haitians for Jesus Christ.

In summary, it is noteworthy to identify at least five patterns that developed during this period.

(1)   Exploration

(2)   Evangelical missions from England, the United States, and Jamaica, represented by the Methodist, Episcopal, Baptist and Seventh-day Adventist denominations.

(3)   A pattern of focus on Evangelism.

(4)   Western missionaries ministering in an animistic setting and a Voodoo worldview unlike their cultural assumptions.

(5)   Missions by immigration in which a profusion of missionaries of "color" brought the gospel to Haiti.

All five patterns somehow contributed to foster a grassroots of Haitian ministry in Haiti. In spite of difficult circumstances, the gospel was proclaimed, people were saved, and churches were planted.

The Extension Phase, 1917 – Present

The second phase of missions (1917- present) started with a sense of stability in Haiti. The socio-political landscape had changed with the American occupation in 1915. Thereafter a proliferation of missions agencies followed.

One hundred and ten (110) agencies (90 Americans, 9 Canadians and 11 other countries) were recorded between 1923 and 2000 (Siewert and Welliver 2001, 325-326, 444; Johnstone

2001), compared to 5 agencies (4 American and 1 English) in the previous century missions (Romain 1986, 41). (See appendices 2, 3, and 4 for details.) However, there seems to be a certain disparity in numbers of agencies in the country.

While foreign missions agencies expanded in Haiti during the second phase (see appendices 2, 3 and 4), the grassroots of indigenous Haitian ministry also flourished throughout the land from 5 in the first period (1816-1916) to at least 42 during the extension phase (see appendix 5).

Hammon Johnson argued that it is almost impossible to know how many denominations there are in Haiti. One reason has to do with conflicting records from the Minister of Cults (87), the U.S. Agency for International Development (USAID) of the United States Department of State (145), and the proliferation of unregistered "freelance missionaries" who traveled to Haiti regularly to do missions work (Johnson 1970, IX). On the other hand, Dr. Jules Casséus reported more than 200 agencies in Haiti according to statistics in 1980 (1997, 173).

In the Southern Peninsula, at the request of Haitian believers who came from Cuba, West Indies Mission (WIM) started a Bible school in 1936 "to train Christian workers" (Heneise 1999, 193). Some years later, a dispensary and many countryside clinics were opened. By 1958, Radio Lumière (*Radio of Light)* was implanted to educate and proclaim the gospel. By 2002, the radio ministry had a network of five AM and one FM broadcasting stations reaching nearly six million people (Barrett, Kurian, and Johnson 2001, 341). In 1963, the churches pertaining to WIM organized themselves into a Haitian mission called Mission Evangelique Baptiste du Sud d'Haiti (MEBSH), or in English, *The Evangelical Baptist Mission Southern of Haiti.* MEBSH Statistics for 2000 showed 407 congregations, 40,000 members, 200 primary schools, 7 secondary schools, 3 vocational centers, 1 school of art, and 1 professional school with more than 100,000 constituents (Johnstone and Mandryk 2001, 299). A Christian university was added in 1992 with 8 divisions.[6]

---

[6]Source: http://www.haiti-reference.com/education/superieur/universites.html

In the North, linked with American Baptist Home Missionary Society (ABHMS), the Convention Baptiste Haitienne (CBH) (or in English, *Haitian Baptist Convention)* was founded in 1924. Then in 1947, an outstanding theological seminary was instituted and became in 1993 the Université Chrétienne Du Nord D'Haiti (UCNH) (in English, *Christian University of North Haiti).* By 1978, various relief activities had been organized by Southern Baptists. CBH estimates for 2000 showed 453 congregations, 84,599 members, 90 primary schools with 20,000 pupils, 15 high schools, 20 vocational centers with a constituency of 300,000" (Johnstone and Mandryk 2001, 299; Heneise 1999, 173-174, 180, 185).

After 1958, the Mission (Eglise) Evangélique d'Haiti (MEH) (in English, *Evangelical Mission of Haiti)* was founded in association with the Oriental Missionary Society (OMS). Among its activities, it produced a vocational Bible school, a medical clinic, church plants, and a radio station (4VEH) to cover the Northern part of Haiti with programs in Creole, French, English, and Spanish (Jeanty 1990, 111; Johnson 1970, 42). Estimated statistics for 2000 showed 20 congregations, 3,000 members and a constituency of 12,000 (Johnstone 2001, CD-ROM).

In the southeastern part, Haitian ministry related to ABHMS founded Ebenezer Baptist Mission. Estimated figures for 2000 showed 125 congregations, 10,000 members, and 20,000 affiliates. (Johnstone 2001, CD-ROM)

In the West, the Unevangelized Field Mission (UFM) merged with World Evangelism Crusade (WEC). In order to train leaders, they started a Bible school in 1943 which was later renamed Séminaire Théologique Evangélique de Port-au-Prince (STEP) later. Churches were organized into the Mission Evangelique Baptiste d'Haiti (Evangelical Baptist Mission of Haiti) which was later changed to Union Evangelique Baptiste d'Haiti (UEBH) (in English, *Union of Baptist Evangelicals of Haiti).* UFM built one hospital, three secondary schools, and even a printing press. UEBH estimated statistics for 2000 showed 420 congregations, 19,000 members, and 38,000 constituents (Johnstone and Mandryk 2001, 299).

In 1946, the church of the Nazarene began their work in Haiti, and their estimated figures for 2000 showed 480 congregations, 78,000 members and 260,000 affiliates, two medical facilities, and one theological school (Johnstone and Mandryk 2001, 299).

The Pentecostal and Charismatic churches greatly contributed to the extension and the dissemination of the gospel in Haiti. In 1928, the church of God (Tennessee) sent Pastor Paulceus Joseph to Haiti as missionary. In 1938, several evangelistic meetings were held resulting in astounding conversions (Romain 1986, 77). In 1944, the mission pioneered in broadcasting live weekly service in Port-au-Prince (Claude Noel, 2003). They organized Bible schools, clinics, and schools throughout the country. Moreover, they initiated days of prayer in the mountains which attracted crowds of people. In fact, they are still growing rapidly, and the Pentecostal and Charismatic estimated statistics for 2000 were substantial. (See appendix 5 for details.)

Conversely, a foreign missions organization, Baptist Haiti Mission (BHM) gathered neglected missions stations initiated by other groups. They organized a National association of these churches "patterned somewhat after that in the United States" (Heneise 1999, 198). BHM statistics for 1998 showed 330 churches and stations, 27,000 members, 100,000 constituents, 331 schools, 60,120 students, 1 hospital, 1 sanitarium, 8 clinics, and contributions to various community development projects.[7]

Though their initial work began in 1879 in Haiti, the Seventh-Day Adventists (SDA) took a new direction in 1905 (Johnson 1970, 46). Their estimated figures for 2000 reported 306 congregations, 213,938 members and 400,000 affiliates, 1 hospital, and 1 university to train pastors and teachers (Johnstone and Mandryk 2001, 299).

Statistics for other Haitian ministries available to the author are listed in appendix 5. Still other ministries, though inaccessible for the purpose of this study, have in one way or another contributed to spreading the gospel in Haiti as well.

---

[7]Source: http://www.bhm.org/ministry/stats.htm

After 1959, Haitian expatriates migrated in great numbers to Europe, the USA, Canada, Latin America, Africa, and Caribbean Islands other than Haiti. As a result, thousands were saved in different places through the preaching of the gospel, and numerous churches were planted by Haitian leaders in places such as New York, Florida, Chicago, Montreal, Guadeloupe, Paris, etc.

In summary, in spite of complex socio-cultural conditions, the gospel moved forward in the second phase with the expansion of foreign missions agencies, the valued support of missionaries, the dedication of Haitian leaders, and a great emphasis on evangelism.

The increase in the percentage of Evangelicals and Pentecostals/Charismatics in the country bore witness to the fact that, although a certain variance exists as to their actual numbers, their work had been taking root in the country during this period. Compared to the first phase in which 0.6 percent (of 2,124,000 Haitians in 1920) was estimated, different percentages of converts were given for the second phase of Evangelical and Pentecostal/Charismatic missions in Haiti. Dr. Jules Casséus reported the outcome of statistics in 1980 at 33.33 percent (Casséus 1997, 173). However, Dr. Fritz Fontus emphasized the outcome of a survey in the capital of Haiti (Port-au-Prince) of 48.3 percent for the age group 18 to 25 in 1996 (Fontus 2001, 90, 82). Furthermore, it is contended that by mid-2000, the percentage for Evangelicals together with Pentecostals, Charismatics, and Great Commission Christians have reached 38.8 percent (Barrett, Kurian, and Johnson 2001, 339). Conversely, Johnstone and Mandryk argued for 22 percent in 2001, though some estimated 30 percent, (Johnstone 2001, CD-ROM). Nonetheless, an interview conducted with the President of MEBSH (2002) reported 40 to 42 percent nationwide. He commented that a study done by World Vision on the island of La Gonave alone indicated 67 percent in that region. Moreover, a survey conducted by MEBSH in a major city of the Southern Peninsula (Les Cayes) reported 67.8 percent. It appears that the percentage of Evangelicals and Pentacostal/Charismatics is constantly on the rise (Jeune, interview by author, 5 November 2002).

Estimated numbers for the Haitian population from 1824 to 2025 are listed in appendix 24. However, the author concurred with Dr. Fritz Fontus and others who argued that in a country akin to Haiti, statistics are ambiguous. Therefore, in this study, the author used an estimated figure of 8.5 million as the Haitian population for 2003, with 38 percent average of Evangelicals and Pentecostals/Charismatics. The remaining percentage of the population was prominently Catholic linked with Voodoo (Romain 1986, 96).

Despite an outstanding multiplication of believers, it would appear however that evangelistic efforts during both phases did not penetrate all strata of the Haitian society. Though the upper class was theoretically Roman Catholic, the apparent absence of a combined effort among Evangelicals and Pentecostals/Charismatics seems to indicate that no deliberate attempt was made to attain them for Christ.

Not many ministries directly focused on the upper class in Haiti. Johnstone and Mandryk (*Operation World,* 300) argued that the elite are the least evangelized of the population. However, Radio Lumière FM station planted the seed with Stereo 92 for more than two decades. Quisqueya Christian School somehow contributed through Christian education. Morning Star Christian Academy apparently did the same. Likewise, churches such as: Eglise de la Communauté Evangelique D'Haiti, Eglise Sur Le Rocher, and Quisqueya Church became a contributing factor as did Jesus Center. Fellowship House in Petion-Ville, led by Don Weaver, was specifically geared toward the upper class. Other ministries not known to the author might lean toward that direction as well. (Chavannes Jeune, interview by author, 5 November 2002; Vladimir Jeune. electronic correspondence, 7 March 2003; Cadet, interview by author, notes, 19 December 2002)

In spite of some positive results that emerged not long ago, much work is yet to be done before the gospel will make significant progress in the upper class sector of the Haitian society.

On the other hand, encouraging steps have been taken by the younger generation among whom 28 GBEUH[8] (IFES) groups have shared their faith with fellow students on university campuses. These efforts have made inroads into the emerging generation of professionals in the country (Johnstone and Mandryk 2001, 300).

Several trends may be noted during this period. First, the increase of foreign missions has also brought a shift in missionary personnel (more white missionaries than ones of color). Second, the majority of the Haitian ministries have been related to the foreign missions which founded them. Third, most efforts were made to reach the lower class of Haiti rather than the upper class. Fourth, the Haitian Church has expanded beyond its borders through the migration of expatriates to different countries as mentioned above. Fifth, Evangelical and Pentecostal/Charismatic Christianity in Haiti increased from 0.6 percent in the first century of missions (1816-1916) in the country with a total population of 2,124,000 in 1920 to a 38 percent average nationwide (with a population of 8,500,000 in 2003). It is obvious to everyone that such a statistical upsurge (37.4 percent) in less than a century is certainly significant. Nonetheless, did this dramatic increase occur without side effects? Were the methods missionaries used in communicating the gospel to Haitians compatible with the local culture? Was the gospel adequately contextualized, or was the Haitian culture overlooked in the process? The answers to these questions cannot be ignored, because they have a vital connection to the development of the missionary vision in the Haitian Church. The next section will explore the philosophy and methodology missionaries used to communicate the gospel message within an animistic context embedded in a Voodoo worldview following Haiti's independence in 1804.

---

[8] GBEUH stands for Groupe Biblique Des Etudiants et des Universitaires d'Haiti and IFES stands for International Fellowship of Evangelical Students. Their purpose is to study the Bible as believers and take the gospel to fellow students on university campuses.

Contemporary Evangelical and Pentecostal/Charismatic Mission Activity in Haiti

Everyone would concur with Edwin L. Frizen, Jr.'s argument in *Seventy-Five Years of IFMA (Interdenominational Foreign Mission Association)"*:

> The greatest challenge facing missions today is the challenge of the unachieved. The challenge of an unfinished task demands that past performance be honestly and thoroughly examined. Every facet of past mission activity must be examined. (Frizen 1992, 428)

Commenting on Frizen's report, Alex Araujo states:

> The task he [Frizen] sets before us is as delicate as it is necessary. Because it is necessary it must be addressed with urgency and zeal; because it is delicate it must be approached with great tact and humility. And the scope of the task is such that it must be faced in community and not in isolation...Re-evaluation will not only document true achievements and bring thanksgiving to God; it will also reveal some painful truths. (Araujo 1993, 362-363)

A review of past performance among Evangelical and Pentecostal/Charismatic foreign mission activities in Haiti must take into account an evaluation of at least three significant factors: (1) the applied philosophy of missions (their belief), (2) the methodology (how they do missions), and (3) the philosophy and methodology transferred to the Haitian church.

1) PHILOSOPHY OF MISSIONS

An examination of missions literature in the Haitian Church determined that the philosophy of missions was classified into Evangelicals and Pentecostals/Charismatics categories.

Evangelicals

In general, Evangelicals believe in world evangelization aimed at persuading the lost to accept the Lord Jesus Christ in obedience to the Great Commission. The author's conversation with former missionaries in Haiti revealed that some foreign missionaries in Haiti did not emphasize Acts 1:8 in their preaching. To the contrary, they neglected to inform the people to go abroad, outside their world, with the message of the gospel. In fact, there was little challenge in that regard, even to ask local pastors or laypeople to pray for missionaries around the world (The Sees, 2000). While evangelism was the primary focus, Evangelical missionaries emphasized the gospel for the whole man.

Pentecostals/Charismatics

Pentecostals/Charismatics shared the same beliefs as the Evangelicals, except for a greater emphasis on the Holy Spirit. Their purpose was stated quite obviously: "the Pentecostals aimed to convert the heathen to Christianity as quickly as possible" (Burgess 2002, 895). McClung defended the Pentecostal position regarding "the experience of Baptism of the Holy Spirit as a requisite provision of power for world evangelization" (Burgess and McGee 1989, 607). Likewise, Pentecostal circles tended to accentuate that healing, speaking in tongues, and exorcism were to go along with the proclamation of the gospel. They believe that signs are attached to the gospel, not to the apostles.

In summary, the philosophy of missions applied by both Evangelical and Pentecostal/Charismatic missionaries revolved around evangelism at a local level. However, when the cultural context and the Voodoo worldview were not given further attention in the communication process, it was then predictable that the missionary vision tantamount to the Gospels and Acts was less likely to be transferred.

In this context it is vital to identify how both categories (Evangelicals and Pentecostals/Charismatics) carried out missions in Haiti. Because of their similarities in methodology, both groups are studied together.

2) METHODOLOGY

In scanning the literature regarding the methodology missionaries applied in Haiti, numerous concerns and practices were associated with their methods. Among the variety of strategy employed, at least two patterns stood out: (1) church planting and (2) leadership training.

Church Planting

In general, church planting grew out of evangelism, which was the primary focus of most missions activity in Haiti. Different methods were used to plant churches. Among them were: house meetings, Bible studies, prayer groups, distribution of literature, visitation, outstations, revival, open-air evangelism, and education. Missionaries started schools and related them to the church for education and evangelism purposes (Jeanty 1990, 60; Kane 1972, 509). Furthermore, they built churches, medical centers, provided compassion ministries, organized community development, and provided subsidies to several national leaders (Heneise 1999, 128). Although this model was more paternalistic than Haitian or incarnational, it still positively contributed to the spread of the gospel throughout Haiti.

Steve Weber and Rosemary Walker commented on serious issues affecting National Churches. Weber wrote in his thesis on church growth in Haiti:

> Another major problem in both the church planting and development activities of the Protestants in Haiti has been the nearly universal endorsement of the "West is Best" supposition. This is seen in the failure to contextualize the type of Protestant Christianity that has been planted in Haiti, as well as in the types of technological approaches used in relief and development." (1980, 59)

On the other hand, Walker discussed the effect of such approach citing a case in South-Central Africa:

> One of the reasons that prevented the church to send out missionaries was the result of overly-autocratic leadership from the part of the missionaries: "Nationals were not included in the decision-making process for many years. They were just told what to do until 1968. The reason for this was paternalism, the idea that "Africans do not know. We know. We have to tell them." Wherever there was a white man, he was in charge--regardless of his age. Missionaries were overly protective. They didn't try to get the nationals involved in the ministry or in decision-making. It was like a master and a servant. (Rosemary E. Walker, *The Communication of a Cross-Cultural Missionary Vision to National Churches* [M.A. Thesis, Columbia Biblical Seminary and Graduate School of Missions, 1993], 56)

Music

After churches are planted, congregations needed songs for worship. Missionaries imported hymns from America and Europe and translated them for the benefit of the Haitian Church.

Exceptions were made of the Pentecostal/Charismatic churches whose various hymns often embodied the contextual situation. Later those hymns were compiled into the Haitian Hymnbook *Chants d'Espérance,* which means *Songs of Hope.* Though "transplanting the church" and its music was not the best option, it is noteworthy to highlight that God used it somehow to keep the National Church up and running.

Dr. Fritz Fontus noted that the hymnbook used by the Haitian Church at large (*Chants d'Espérance*) sells 24,000 copies yearly. The great majority of the 610 hymns represent a Western mindset. The author (of this thesis) realized that many of these songs were not designed for a Haitian context. For instance, "Whiter than Snow" (# 65 French in the Haitian hymnbook) has been sung for decades, even until today. But most people have yet to realize that this song was not written for a tropical environment. The concept "snow" does not connect with the day-to-day Haitian reality. Therefore, the author asserts that this song could be contextualized to reflect the Haitian context.

Nonetheless, a lack of consideration for the cultural context and the Haitian worldview was unmistakable in the translation process. For instance, music styles, as well as instruments Haitians used prior to conversion, were replaced by Western instruments in almost every category. In the woodwind and brass section, "bamboo" was replaced by saxophone, clarinet, trumpet, and flute. In the strings group, banjo (which is from African origin) was supplanted by guitar and bass. In the percussion area: cymbal and related native instruments were superseded by drum, piano, and organ, etc. The rhythms as well as the music styles were unseated by more traditional Western and European styles.

Likewise, Fontus explained the missionary methodology this way:

> The first method is to transplant the church, as it existed in the mother or sending church, to the field. It leads to the building of churches which are carbon copies of the sending churches, depriving the young churches of any

51

possibility of developing their own theological thinking. (Fontus 2001, 126, 142)

To illustrate the case, Steve Weber used the Church of the Nazarene as a case in point:

> The reason the Church of the Nazarene sends cross-cultural missionaries is to plant the Church of the Nazarene in other countries. In doctrine, polity, and literally every other dimension possible, the Haitian Church is a replica of the sending church in the United States...The Nazarenes are attempting to plant a reproduction of the U.S.-based church. (Weber 1980, 97, 101)

That cultural replacement approach led several intellectual leaders and theologians alike and even religious leaders to make a case for the reassertion of the Haitian culture. According to their perspectives, at conversion the Haitian believer was expected to embrace the Western culture at the expense of his or her own cultural identity. The inescapable conclusion that emerged from that premise was that Haitian believers came into a gospel that was foreign to them. Therefore, they pleaded for the reintegration of the Haitian cultural identity, or particularly for the haitianization of the Haitian churches, no matter the outcome would be.

Those who argued in favor of the haitianization of the Haitian Church tended to believe that Voodoo in its actual practice should coexist with the gospel. To do otherwise, from their perspective, would be to deprive the Haitian Church of its cultural heritage. In so doing, the advocates of that view brought back on the table the tension that still exists between the gospel and culture. Acts 15 is a perfect case in point. This conflict has been around at least since the first century Church and will not disappear anytime soon. Furthermore, the Lausanne 1974 Gathering and Willobrank Consultation (Bermudes) were very concerned about this conflict and had addressed the issue.

The author (of this thesis) strongly believes that the born-again Christian should not eradicate his cultural heritage at conversion, nor should the missionary do it.   However, in the conversion process, the new convert needs to reevaluate everything pertaining to his or her cultural patrimony in light of the gospel (new faith) and live accordingly under the Lordship of Jesus Christ. Otherwise, it would be akin to accepting the predominance of the Haitian culture at the expense of the gospel, or to agree to a syncretistic lifestyle contrary to the true nature of the gospel itself.

The inability to see the gospel as different from human cultures has been the Achilles heel of modern Christian missions. Histories of missions around the world have reported that during the colonial era and beyond, many missionaries imposed on the nationals their imported culture because of ethnocentrism. Haiti is no exception. That was a wrong approach, as revealed by the devastating effects that followed. This methodology often created a form of Christo-paganism – a syncretism between the new faith and the old beliefs, or recidivism. To avoid this problem of syncretism, missionaries should not continue to crush, replace, nor despise the host culture in which they are trying to communicate the gospel message, as has been the case in the past.

On the other hand, those who made a case for the compatibility of Voodoo with the gospel -- in other words the haitianization of the Haitian Church (according to their perspectives) -- in reality are pleading for acceptance of the old way. It is essential to bear in mind that no culture shape or form is pure in and by itself. There is no neutrality in any culture. Therefore, the gospel belongs to no particular culture. Culture cannot supersede the gospel. The latter is expressed in and through cultures and thus transcends them all.

What the advocates of the haitianization of the Haitian Church probably failed to understand (as already explained in chapter 1, "Theological and Biblical Basis of the Study") is the corruption of the human race. The Bible highlights many times over, particularly in the Epistle to the Romans, that there is universal sinfulness, guilt, and condemnation of the human race. As a result, all human cultures have inherited "ingredients," modus operandi, and/or rituals that were evil and contrary to Scriptures. The Haitian culture is not exempt.

When considering the issue of culture in relation to the gospel, if anyone refuses to accept Paul's theological argument in Romans 5, it is akin to denying at least the doctrines pertaining to Christology, Pneumatology, and Harmatiology. Those who reject Paul's fundamental principles of universal sinfulness in fact believe that "there are no absolutes" and consequently embrace relativism. Therefore, instead of making a case for the haitianization of the Haitian Church, the author (of this thesis) is pleading for critical contextualization of the gospel in the Haitian Church (and elsewhere using the same approach) and not the opposite of replacing local culture or of allowing local culture to supersede the gospel.

Critical contextualization starts with the Bible as the ultimate and definitive authority for Christian beliefs and practices. It continues with the collection of information about the old way. That leads to diligent study of biblical teachings about different issues, evaluation of the old in the light of biblical teachings, and ultimately to creation of a new contextualized Christian practice. Nonetheless, whatever shape or form that critical contextualization would take in the Haitian Church, it cannot absolutely be incompatible or in contradiction with Scriptures.

Former missionary in Haiti Edwin Walker, as a result of 23 years of ministry in Haiti's animistic context, commented on the importance of worldview discipleship relating to the Haitian Church. He said:

> One of the most difficult yet essential tasks in cross-cultural church planting is to embed a consistent biblical worldview or conceptual framework replacing false ones. Without intentional worldview disciple making accompanied by the supernatural illumination of the Holy Spirit, weak, unhealthy, and sterile churches will most likely be the results of our church-planting efforts....
>
> In the Voodoo worldview there is no concept of sin because everything one does is caused by a spirit over which the person has no ultimate control...an individual is not

responsible for his conduct and all that happens to him comes from the spirits that are arbitrary which lead to fatalism and to poverty....

When someone hears the gospel even when communicated in their language with accuracy and clarity, their worldview determines to a large degree how they understand or misunderstand the message... The meaning of a passage in the Bible is often distorted because the reader interprets the passage in the light of his worldview...If people maintain their secular and animistic worldviews although being converted, it is easy to revert back into old pre-conversion beliefs and patterns...Therefore to fail to do adequate worldview disciple-making produces weak churches which often lead to rapid recidivism....

All too often cross-cultural missionaries from Western secular cultures have never fully replaced the secular dichotomistic worldview of their own culture with a consistent biblical worldview that is holistic...No area of the church-planting task is more important than this one. (Walker, *The Importance of Worldview*, 2002)

If the critical contextualization is done properly as the church is planted, the National Church will develop its own theology by maintaining a channel of communication between the contemporary culture and the Bible itself. As a result, genuine transformation will occur, and Haitian believers will be enabled to reach the world for Christ with the message of the Great Commission. (Hiebert 2001, 52-56; 183-192)

Leadership Training

At first, as people got saved in Haiti and churches were planted and songs translated, a theological education was not required to lead a congregation. In an attempt to remedy the situation, training the Nationals to lead the Church became imperative. Several missions organized their own Bible schools, equipping pastors with the focus to reach their fellow Haitians for Christ.

In the Southern Peninsula, West Indies Mission (WIM) started a Bible school in 1936. In the Northern part, American Baptist Home Missionary Society (ABHMS) instituted a theological seminary as well as the Oriental Missionary Society (OMS), which had a vocational Bible school. On the Western side, the Unevangelized Field Mission (UFM) started a Bible school in 1943. The Pentecostals and Charismatics, the Seventh-Day Adventists, and the Church of the Nazarene did the same. Recent statistics report about 20 Bible schools/seminaries and several Theological Education by Extension (TEE) programmes seeking to meet the needs for training in Haiti. (Johnstone and Mandryk 2001, 300)

In the process of providing training, several Bible schools and seminaries did not teach a contextualized missions courses or the Great Commission per se, or how to organize missions conferences. James W. Sutherland observed the same trend in the African American (AFAM) church setting as well: "Little or nothing is taught on CC[9] ministries in AFAM Seminaries or Bible Institutes that prepare AFAM Pastors and Christian Workers. The emphasis is to reach 'YOUR OWN' people!" (Sutherland 1998, 162-163)

Conversely, others, such as Edwin Walker, with great honesty and transparence, provided insight about the struggle to relate to the host culture so different from one's own context. The author is grateful to retired missionary in Haiti Edwin Walker, who granted him permission to use his unpublished material. Walker said:

I grew up in a context that held a modernistic worldview. Once I received Christ as my Lord and Savior and began to study the Bible, I quickly began to understand that modernism was opposed to my new faith. Nevertheless, I did not realize how deeply I continued to be influenced by

---

[9] CC = cross-cultural

the modernistic worldview until I became immersed in the animistic Voodoo culture of Haiti. To my shame, it took about 12 years in that context before I began to have any real insight as to what was going on in the Haitian mind as I was trying to teach the gospel or anything else. I found in many areas what I was thinking I was teaching and what my disciples were understanding was often very different. I did not understand their conceptual framework. (Even in methodology I was wrong because they learned through narrative communication and I was far too long trying to teach by using Western logical reasoning). (Edwin Walker, December 2002, 12-13)

Thus it appears that in spite of tremendous efforts missionaries made, Haitian pastors were not adequately trained to take the gospel to the nations of the world[10]. The unawareness of cultural conditions and the teaching method missionaries used to educate pastors have become contributing factors that created a sense of confusion about the Great Commission in its global perspective. Therefore, whatever the pastors' understanding of the missionary mandate so was that of the Haitian Church.

In summary, missionaries trained nationals to focus on soul winning in the local context. The lack of biblical teaching on missions, and the partial contextualization of the gospel message in an animistic environment embedded with a Voodoo worldview are illustrations of some factors that have contributed to limit the global vision of the National Church. Likewise, the nationals were not adequately trained to take over when missionaries would be gone. Examples of this model were BHM, OMS and other agencies in Haiti. In all certainty, their methodology left its stamp on the Haitian churches' lack of global perspective.

---

[10] Studies done in evangelical churches in Latin American countries seem to show similar trends, such as in church numerical growth and retention yet with an absence of discipleship (Escobar 2003, 288-289).

3) PHILOSOPHY AND METHODOLOGY
TRANSFERRED

Undoubtedly, many would agree that the missionaries' philosophy and methodology were applied with the primary intent to spread the gospel, plant churches, and meet the spiritual and physical needs of the Haitian people. A primary example of this approach that set a great precedent was that used by the Methodists. They first built schools linked to churches, which became a pattern for later generations. Since missionaries often administered compassion ministries and provided subsidies to national leaders, and since a trained pastor was not mandatory to lead a church, this approach became a replica for the Haitian Church under the same circumstances.

While churches were built on behalf of the national fellowship or in cooperation with them, in general a missionary's paternalistic approach unwittingly cultivated a dependence mentality or ultimately led to picture the National Church as a "welfare church."[11] In this regard, Johnson commented:

> Foreign sponsored institutions of social assistance have other deleterious effects on the growth of the church. By their emphasis, they have created serious misunderstandings as to the nature of the gospel. They have taught the Haitians that the gospel involves only *receiving* of someone else's bounty. The gospel as something to be shared is ignored or minimized. The intended object lesson of Christian love is misunderstood. Instead, the Haitians see the gospel as involving *receiving* education, *receiving* medical help, *receiving* relief from vodun, and *receiving* Christ as things of a kind. The enforced dependence can only lead to problems…The

---

[11] The author of this book is raising a very penetrating question with regards to the labeling of the Haitian Church comparable to the welfare church: *Who has created that welfare church?* To say the least, certainly not the indigenous Church.

present financial situation of the *Haitian* [emphasis mine] churches is the result of policies adopted in the early years of the establishment of the Protestant churches and maintained through the years. (Johnson 1970, 66, 77)

That dependence approach appeared to have been the result of a lack of sustained effort to teach the National Church to be self-supportive. Some missionaries already foresaw the devastating effect of this practice. Sadly, little has yet been done to overcome this dependency (Heneise 1999, 139). Johnson confirmed the existence of the problem:

Most missionaries and many Haitian Church leaders recognize that foreign subsidy constitutes a problem for church growth. No one is quite sure how to deal with the problem....For better or worse the churches rely heavily on subsidies....The great need is for the Haitian churches to be taught stewardship. When I mentioned this to missionaries and pastors, I was usually referred to materials teaching tithing. I found no materials available in Haiti in either French or Creole that dealt with the whole concept of stewardship. (Johnson 1970, 78-79)

Considering the existence of such an inaccurate, ingrained view of the gospel, one could infer that this dilemma not only affected church growth per se, but more importantly limited the financial capacity of the Haitian Church to carry out its mission to the nations of the world as spelled out in the Gospels and Acts.

In summary, under difficult circumstances, foreign missionaries were tremendously used by God for the spread of the gospel in Haiti. Likewise, their kindheartedness to provide social assistance and sponsorship did contribute to the advancement of God's kingdom in Haiti. A single but striking example spoke for itself (37.4 percent increase in less than a century). On the other hand, the philosophy and methodology transferred without adequate contextualization of the gospel message created involuntarily a dilemma which often made the gospel foreign to the Haitian Church.

Both Paul G. Hiebert and David Hesselgrave commented on the issue of worldview and culture. Hiebert wrote:

> Each culture has its own worldview, or fundamental way of looking at things. If this is so, cross-cultural communication at the deepest level is possible only when we understand the world views of the people to whom we minister. It also means that people will understand the gospel from the perspective of their own world view....The "foreignness" of the gospel along with syncretism were the result of the rejection of contextualization (the denial of the old customs) and uncritical contextualization. Both categories lead to consequences. On one hand, rejection of contextualization led to misunderstanding of Christianity, and the old cultural ways "go Underground." Conversely, the uncritical contextualization disregarded that there are corporate and cultural sins. Sin can be found in institutions and practices of a society....The Gospel calls not only individuals but societies and cultures to change. Contextualization must mean the communication of the gospel in ways the people understand, but that also challenge them individually and corporately to turn from their evil ways." (Hiebert 2001, 21, 184-185)

A similar assessment of the worldview dilemma led Hesselgrave to say:

> Missionaries need to learn to communicate Christ to respondents in terms of their (the respondents') way of viewing the world, their way of thinking, their way of expressing themselves in language, their way of acting,...their way of deciding future courses of action. (Hesselgrave 1991, 184)

Haitian Missions Activity

In this section, the author presents how the Haitian leaders perceived and evaluated the missionaries' philosophy and methodology and came to their own philosophy and methodology of missions.

PERCEPTION AND EVALUATION OF MISSIONARIES' PHILOSOPHY AND METHODOLOGY

In general, it seemed there was confusion with missions as a concept for the Haitians. For some, missions referred only to "overseas ministries," while others perceived it as exclusively evangelization of Haitians or perhaps as compassion ministries. This confusion or misunderstanding appeared to be the result of missionaries' teaching Acts 1:8 only in part and inattention to the cultural context and the Haitian worldview. Nationals were apparently persuaded by some missionaries in their teaching on Acts 1:8 that it meant that local believers should reach their "Jerusalem" (their own people), while "Judea, Samaria and the end of the earth" became the agency task" (Jeune, 2002). In fact, missionary vision in a global perspective in essence was not communicated to the Haitian Church (Jeanty, 2000).

Likewise, even when mission conferences were organized in some parts of the country, they often revolved uniquely around soul-winning with a national overtone. Similarly, since missionaries generously responded to the needs of the Haitian people (church building, schools, clinics, compassions ministries, subsidies, community development, and so forth), Haitian believers equated the generosity of the missionaries to missions. To put it another way, the National Church had difficulty dissociating missions from meeting physical needs. They did not perceive both components as mutually exclusive. Because missions was mistakenly understood in the Haitian Church as primarily limited to the local or national level, many people (church leaders and laypeople alike) apparently saw little motivation to get involved in world missions.

Furthermore, some foreign agencies in harmony with different Haitian missions focused their evangelistic efforts onto specific regions within the country such as CBH in the North, UEBH in West and Northwest, MEBSH mostly in the South, and Ebenezer in the Southeast. The Haitians abroad who organized different trips to the country often perceived that endeavor as a regional vision. For instance, those living abroad who came from the North or the Northeast of Haiti had the tendency to regroup into a church on foreign soil. When they organized short-term trips to Haiti, they often went to their respective locality (Jeune, 2002). Needless to say such view of the Great Commission was incompatible to Jesus' approach.

Since local pastors were trained to evangelize their own people through the lens of the Western worldview, believers came to a limited understanding of the meaning of the Great Commission as Jesus intended it to be. This seems evident by the great disproportion of Haitian missionaries reaching out to their countrymen in contrast to the few Haitian missionaries reaching out to other nations. Therefore, nationals perceived the vision transmitted to the Haitian Church as only *local and limited* instead of comprehensive in nature.

HAITIAN PHILOSOPHY AND
METHODOLOGY OF MISSIONS

Various Haitian missions used outstations to plant churches throughout the country in the twentieth century. Schools were added to congregations to educate, evangelize, and create employment for church members and -- to some degree – to support church ministry. The National Church and Haitian missions practiced a holistic approach to missions often supported by foreign funds. Likewise, they linked missions with receiving from missionaries or getting their physical needs met. The

National Church and Haitian missions assumed they could not get involved specifically in overseas missions because of their poverty.

Since missionaries apparently did not challenge the National Church to reach the world (using Acts 1:8), the Haitian Church understood the missionary vision as tantamount to reaching out to their own people (preaching to Haitians in Haiti or abroad). One foreign missionary who was part of the HMC in Evanston e-mailed the author regarding this research:

> There seemed to be only a few people who really had the vision....I didn't get a sense that the people in the church, other than those I mentioned, really cared about going back to Haiti or anywhere else in the world. It seemed they were content to reach out only in their own backyards. Hopefully this has changed since I was there!

As already noted, the Haitian Church came to the conclusion that they could receive missionaries but were not ready to engage in worldwide missions (Jeune, 2002). For instance, constituencies of particular Haitian missions gave a disconcerting reaction when they received a report in which financial support was sent to Haitian missionaries abroad. They tended to justify their attitude by the fact that most pastors in Haiti did not have a monthly salary and not enough to live by. How could Haitian missions have the courage to send financial support to Haitian missionaries overseas? According to their thinking, it should be the other way around.

Pastors belonging to some Haitian missions were not interested in motivating their congregations to support mission work (Casséus, 2002). Others tried to do so but without great success. The author's experience bore witness to the fact that during more than two decades of attending church in Haiti, he did not have any recollection of ever hearing a single sermon on missions or on the Great Commission from a global perspective, nor did he hear foreign missionaries or National leaders biblically teaching the congregants to financially support world missions. What was done in some churches revolved around an additional offering collected once a month for missions, but the majority of the congregants did not understand what missions was and which missionary or missions organization would receive the offering. The outcome of this lack of information contributed to making the missionary mandate in its universal sense an abstract concept to Haitian believers.

Not long ago, when the Haitian churches or organizations sent national missionaries, the great majority went to serve their own people in Haiti or to Haitians living elsewhere. The lack of administrative structure and neglect in caring for the missionaries in the field was a contributing factor leading some missionaries to become independent (Jeune, 2002; Walker, 2003). Furthermore, mostly when the Haitian churches abroad organized evangelistic outreaches in Haiti, they replicated intuitively what they learned from the pioneers, namely: to give away clothes, food, medication, and the like and thus meeting people's physical needs.

The Haitian philosophy of missions was more likely to reflect the idea of home missionaries being deployed by local missions such as CBH, UEBH, MEBSH, and others to evangelize and plant churches within the country. Likewise, some Haitians returned home from abroad as missionaries for full-time ministry (such as the Cadets and the Esperances).

At the end of 20th century, some Haitian groups from abroad, alongside many urban Haitian churches of North America (in New York, Boston, Florida, Chicago, Montreal, and elsewhere) organized short-term trips to Haiti. Overall, they duplicated the same approach foreign missionaries used. They often organized clinics, gave food, and subsidized schools, churches, orphanages and other related programs. These different components associated with the preaching of the gospel responded to a great need and appeared appropriate and harmless.

These short-term trips to Haiti were often colored as missionary work, but in reality, some appeared to relate to compassion ministries more than evangelism-discipleship. Nonetheless, they had ramifications to a certain degree for the spread of the gospel. For instance, many Haitian churches organized short-term trips to Haiti from the New York area. Among them were Eglise Baptiste d'Expression Française de Brooklyn (since 1989) with 50 to 85 believers with Pastor Jean Baptiste Thomas. Eglise Baptiste du Rédempteur d'expression Française did the same with an average of 40 believers (since 1997) with Pastor Jamil Georgeon. From the Boston area, Eglise Baptiste Missionnaire de Boston often organized two trips per year to Haiti with Pastor Soliny Vedrine. Other churches did the same. Eglise Baptiste Missionnaire de Boston along with other people from different places organized an evangelistic crusade once a year to Haitians in the Bahamas (since 1996). Numerous churches and groups in Florida did the same. Among them were: New Hope ministries with (Maude Morin); ACARAP (Action Chrétienne à la recherche des âmes perdues); Eglise Bethany (Pastor Devil Legrand); Eglise Emmanuel; Eglise Evangélique Baptiste Béthel (Pastor Felix St-Louis). From Chicago, Eglise Haïtienne Missionnaire Du Nord went to Haiti for a short-term trip in 1999 with Pastor Pierre R. Cadet, Pastor Frantz Lacombe, Sylvie Désané, Margalie Théodore, Nicole JeanPois, Léonie Médard, and Bien-Aimé Jeanty. From Montréal, Eglise Nouvelle Jerusalem's Choir went with Pastor Sauveur Jean Baptiste. Other churches such as La Bible Parle did the same. (Thomas, interview by author, notes, 14 October 2002 ; Georgeon, interview by author, notes, 14 October 2002; Vedrine, interview by author, 28 June 2002; Jeune, interview by author, 5 November 2002)

The author followed this same pattern during his missions trip to Haiti in 1999. Likewise, he acknowledged the necessity to have compassion for others and to meet their physical needs as much as possible (as Jesus did in Matthew 14:13-21; Mark 6:32-44; Luke 9:10-17; John 6:1-15, and so forth).

Nonetheless, what the author is trying to underline here is the effect that material ingredients, associated with the preaching of the gospel, generates in people's minds. It can lead people to coming to the gospel just for physical and temporal benefits, not because they were spiritually hungry. A case in point was found in John 6: 22-66. As a result, there must be balance and appropriate education and admonition when the preaching of the gospel comes to be associated with material elements. Otherwise, the Church might end up making more converts than genuine disciples, missing the goal of achieving what Jesus commanded.

Some Haitian missionaries show recognition of the geographical instruction of the Great Commission. Notably, among the Haitian churches abroad, *Eglise Baptiste d'expression Française de Brooklyn* expanded its outreach to countries such as: St-Martin, the Bahamas, the Dominican Republic, Switzerland, France, England, and Germany (Thomas 2002).

Information available to the author pointed out that the Evangelistic movement was galvanized at the national level with organizations such as: Haitian Evangelical Crusade Association (HECA) in Florida, founded in 1986 (Jean Baptiste 2002); Vision Missionnaire Mondiale (VMM) (in English, *World Missionary Vision*) founded in 1995 in Haiti (Jeune 2002); Vision globale pour le Protestantisme dans le milieu Haitien (VGPMH) (in English, *Global Vision for the Protestantism in Haitian Milieu)*, http//:www.Vision globale.org, founded in 1998 (Vedrine 2002). All three were primarily Haitian-focused ministries.

Each one of these organizations had a specific focus. Founded by Pastor Matthieu Jean Baptiste in Florida, HECA was an interdenominational organization with an Evangelico-social purpose toward Haitians. VMM's purpose was to organize evangelistic crusades among Haitians in the Caribbean, North America, and Europe. VMM was founded by Dr. Chavannes Jeune and Radio Lumière in Haiti. VGPMH was founded by Dr. Soliny Vedrine in 1998 as a forum for key Haitian leaders to discuss, evaluate, and understand the accomplishment of Protestantism in the Haitian Church. Their first forum was held in Florida with 105 people in attendance. The next was scheduled for November 11-14, 2003, in Florida with 300 expected to attend. (Baptiste, interview by author, 15 October 2002; Jeune, interview by author, 5 November 2002; Vedrine, interview by author, tape recording, 28 June 2002)

Moreover, Christian seminaries and Bible schools in the country apparently were not effectively equipped to meet the challenge in leadership training with a global perspective. Though some encouraged that vision, it did not seem to materialize now.

Interviews with former professors of Bible school, a Christian university president, a Haitian missions leader, a former seminary student, and missionaries in Haiti revealed that many students coming out of seminary apparently lack the global vision. Even though an established place was given to missiology, the curriculum and texts used for this discipline were somewhat inadequate. (Jeanty 2000, 27; Casséus, interview by author, 14 October 2002; Jeune, interview by author, 5 November 2002; Jean O. Lilite, interview by author, 21 October 2002; Cadet, interview by author, 19 December 2002)

Other initiatives known to the author took the gospel to different territories (see appendix 23 for further details). For instance, with the Baptists, Dr. Fritz Fontus went to Africa in 1965 as a missionary for 14-1/2 years to the "Ivory Coast, Cameroun, Burkina Faso, Mali, Senegal, Niger, the Central African Republic, Zaire, Benin, Reunion, Madagascar, Mauritius, and Togo" (Fontus 2001, 91). In 1969, Felix Saint Louis went to Guadeloupe for 11 years. In 1977, Thelemaque Desamour went to Comoro Island, Kenya, and Zaire for 2 years. In 1989, Marc Hancy Charles went to Africa and France for 4 years. In 1990, Marie Myrtha Eleazard went to Reunion (in Africa) for 3 months. From 1994 to 2001, Lesly Milord ministered on a short-term basis in different countries such as the Dominican Republic, Croatia (3 weeks), Mali (3 weeks), and Honduras (54 weeks) (Jean Pierre 2003). In 1995, Edner Jeanty went to Zaire (in Africa) for 18 months. In 1997, four missionaries (Jonias Destine, Ronald Jean Louis, Adelson Jean Simon, and Nanette Desvarennes) went to Sudan for 6 weeks. In 2000, Jean W. Firmin and Margery Berthole went respectively to Chad and Ghana for 3 months and 2 weeks. In 2003, Pierre R. Cadet went to Togo and Benin for 2 weeks, and Fredrine Louis and Suzie Destournel went to Madagascar in the same year for 3 months each. Many other Baptist missionaries went to other places such as the Caribbean Islands, Europe, Africa, and America and ministered for many years (Saint Louis 2003; Desarmour 2003; Charles 2003; Eleazard 2003; Jeanty 2003; Destine 2003; Firmin 2003; Berthole 2003; Cadet 2003; Louis 2003; and Destournel 2003).

In 1967, along with the Seventh-Day Adventists, Dr. Roland Joachin began his ministry abroad, particularly in Gabon and Cameroun. During his 29 years of work, he was responsible for the Central African region and became President of the University of Ghana. In 1972, Michel Cherenfant went to Cameroun, Gabon, Chad, Equatorial Guinea, Ivory Coast, and Togo, for 12 years. In 1976, Joses L. Joseph went to different places in Africa for 12 years. In 1983, Pierre Deshommes went to Ethiopia, Central Africa, Chad, the Congo, Equatorial Guinea, Cameron, and Guinea for 8 years. In 1980, Simon Honore went to countries such as Burundi and Rwanda (Africa) for 6 years. In 1984, Disciples and Nino Amertil went to Zaire for 3 years. In 1989, Max Jose Pierre went to Gabon and Cameroun, for 12 years. Many other SDA missionaries such as: Fritz Gerard Noel, Claude Celicourt, Jerame Osee, Anorld Corbien, Joseph Boutros, Jacques Noel, Dr. Fatal, Edner Corbier, Emmanuel Gustave, Jonas Lamour, Deus Cheri, and Alcega Janito ministered in different places in the Caribbean as well as in Africa and other places, serving for many years (Joachin 2003; Deshommes 2003; Honore 2003; Amertil 2003).

With the Pentecostals, the following missionaries undertook missions. Beginning in 1969, Pastor Euguene Germain ministered in Guadeloupe for many years. Beginning in 1970 and continuing to the present, George Morissette has been ministering in various capacities through short-term trips to different places such as: Cameroon, Equatorial Guinea, Ghana, Senegal, Gabon, and Belgium. Marie Lourdes Noel also engaged short-term missions overseas; however, the details of her work were not available at the time this work was published. In 1976, Andre and Manolie Marcelin ministered in Chad for 2 to 3 years. (Morissette 2003)

With the independent (Protestants), in 2002 and 2003, Pierre Vericain went to the Congo and Rwanda for 2 to 3 weeks.

Some other Haitians served in short-term missions with Operation Mobilization and other missions Agencies (Jeanty, 2002). Even though she did not make it to Chad (Africa), it was worth mentioning that after being appointed to the African Inland Mission (AIM) in her sixties, Annacia Désir was called home to heaven on March 2003 (Walker, 2003). A group of five to seven Haitian believers in the Midwest (USA) are planning a trip to Africa in 2004. Finally, there might be other Haitians involved in cross-cultural missions unknown to the author that could have enhanced this study.

In summary, the Haitian Church has made significant progress at the dawn of inaugurating the beginning of our third Century of independence as of January 1st, 2004. One milestone is the statistical measurement showing 37.4 percent increase in Evangelical and Pentecostal/Charismatic Christianity within Haiti (apart from those who lived abroad) in less than a century. This is God preparing the Haitian Church for something good. In that sense, the future looks bright for the Haitian believers in Haiti and elsewhere. Consequently, there is hope for the years to come. The gospel has been proclaimed throughout the country and has been making inroads on different soils. This new awareness for overseas missions as well as homeland endeavors seems to be emerging in Haiti as well as abroad. This shows the desire of the Haitian people to contribute to the fulfillment of the Great Commission worldwide.

Despite progress, the local churches have a great need for sound biblical teaching that specifically addresses missions before they can embrace unreservedly the missionary mandate in its global perspective. The churches abroad that have emerged in a different cultural, socio-economical, and religious context from the mother Church (Haiti), can become a greater asset for that endeavor if they are in tune with the reality of God's greater purpose. Numerous resources are already available and more are set to come.

Studying the Implications

Data from the literature reviewed demonstrated that the Haitian Church has made gigantic steps from its inception to the present. The growing percentage of Evangelical and Pentecostal/ Charismatic churches in Haiti and abroad is an example of such numerical growth. This growth is due in part to the efforts of foreign missionaries who contributed greatly to the extension of the gospel in Haiti. The Haitian people have a profound sense of appreciation and admiration for these missionaries. The author is indebted to God for their dedication and labor. They were used as catalysts to plant seeds that have already emerged in some areas.

Yet, considering Jesus' overall missions approach as presented by the Gospel writers, the answer to the question raised at the beginning of this chapter has become obvious to the author. That question, again is this: *What factors that can cause confusion about Christ's missionary mandate have specific ramifications within the Haitian Church?* Dr. Fritz Fontus has summarized the state of affairs of the Haitian Church this way:

> Almost all the scholars who have written on the subject have recognized the weaknesses of the methods which were used in the past, in spite of the spectacular results these methods have made possible. The Gospel was brought to non-Christians wrapped in the Western cultural traditions ….In many Third World countries Christianity is an intruder. It has not been sufficiently contextualized. Haiti is no exception. (Fontus 2001, 1)

Contrary to the incident reported in Acts 15 with the Gentile church in Antioch, in terms of cultural sensitivity or contextualization of the gospel message, the Haitian Church did not fully receive the same treatment. Therefore, the gospel appeared foreign to the National Church. The "foreignness" of the gospel has created to some extent a domino effect that shaped the Haitian Church in at least four ways: (1) numerical growth, (2) spiritual shallowness, (3) reversion, and (4) the impeding of its missionary vision.

In chapter 1, the author attempted to demonstrate that the Great Commission was modeled after Jesus' global vision, which put identical emphasis on disciple-making and evangelism and equal weight on geographical structure (whether local, regional, or abroad). Since foreign missionaries failed to adequately disciple their converts, the meaning of Acts 1:8 was understood or misunderstood in light of the animistic context and the Haitian worldview. Therefore, this misunderstanding has contributed to helping the Haitians to reach their own people first but has impeded their progress in attaining the world for Christ.

It was then concluded that five factors stood out from among those causing confusion about the missionary mandate that had specific ramifications with the Haitian Church, or that contributed to the restrictive view of the Great Commission in the National Church:

(1) Lack of adequate biblical teaching on missions

(2) Inadequate applied theology and methodology

(3) Deficiency in missions exposure both in seminary and in the church

(4) Inadequate contextualization of the gospel

(5) Lack of challenge from missionaries and National Church pastors persuading Haitian believers to get involved in world missions

What were the issues that can facilitate the National Church to reach the next level of ministry as to fully embrace the global perspective of the missionary mandate? In *The Next Christendom,* Philip Jenkins argued that "Over the past century, however, the center of gravity in the Christian world shifted inexorably southward, to Africa, Asia, and Latin America. This trend will continue apace in coming years" (2002, 2). If intentional about contributing to the fulfillment of the Great Commission, the Haitian Church has to position itself to take up the global level of involvement as the Spirit draws Haitian believers to reach out to the non-Western world with the gospel message.

In order to prepare for global mission, the following three issues, among others, need to be highlighted:

(1) *Growing and Sharing the Global Missions Vision:* The vision of the Great Commission in its global perspective

must be communicated in every imaginable way possible in Haiti and abroad. The Haitian Church has become more than ever in great need of a "serious vision-giving and vision-building mission education." Dr. Chavannes Jeune acknowledged that it was yet to be done at a national level (Jeune, 2002). Even though foreign missionaries apparently did not communicate that universal vision, they planted the seed of the gospel in the heart of the Haitian Church. Consequently, the nationals bear the responsibility now to nurture that embryo and bring it to its culmination at an international level. That is the task entrusted to VIGCOM Ministries, a Haitian faith-based ministry (see appendix 27 and the website www.vigcom.org for further information). The emerging generation can be used as a catalyst to materialize that vision alongside the previous generations.

(2) *Focusing Outward Instead of Inward:* The Haitian Church needs to transform its perception from a mission field to a sending field. Many efforts were made by Haitian missions to place missionaries in different fields, but a lot of work remains yet to be done in this area to make missions effective. However, the resurgence of such endeavors can be short-lived if isolated cases are not transformed into formal structures that have the capacity to carry out a greater impact for the Haitian Church. For instance, in 1987, Luis Bush declared that "Latin America is no longer a mission field; but instead is a missionary force." Ten years later, the Latin American countries sent 4000 missionaries to work in cross-cultural settings while at the same time creating 400 mission agencies (U.S. Center for World Mission 2001, 97). If the Haitian churches are intentional about global missions, they need to tap their resources and work together for that purpose. One example might be to create a network of human and financial resources available in Haiti and abroad to match the actual need of

the field of interest. Haitian churches must take concrete actions such as creating agencies conducive to that goal and partnering with other churches to make that a reality as was done not only in America, but through many sending agencies around the world. (Visit www.vigcom. org for more details.)

(3) *Developing a Sense of "Wholeness":* Contrary to the "dependence" mentality created by paternalism associated with subsidies, the Haitian Church needs to change its way of thinking regarding foreign missions. Instead of continuously receiving subsidies from abroad, one alternative for the national leaders and churches might be to pattern themselves after Melvin Hodges' depiction of the New Testament model to become churches that are "self-propagating...self-governing... self-supporting" (Hodges 1976, 12). (See www.vigcom. org for materials.)

Some efforts have already been made to create agencies that would facilitate the deployment of missionaries from the Caribbean to the nations of the world. Edwin Walker, former missionary in Haiti with World Team, organized different meetings both in Haiti and in the Caribbean, laying the foundation for a non-Western agency. As a result, a Caribbean alliance was created in 1998 with countries where World Team ministered, such as: Guadeloupe, Guyane, St-Lucie, St-Croix, and Haiti. The purpose of the alliance was to recruit, train, and deploy missionaries around the world. Their effort seemed to bear fruit since they apparently seconded three missionaries to other mission agencies. On the other hand, it appeared that other Haitian missions organization such as MEBSH, UEBH, Church of God, Nazarene and others were attempting to put their hands together to create a national agency in Haiti. It may be too early to make any value judgment regarding the validity of this organization. (Edwin Walker, "Global Sharing of Resources: Special Task Force Study Edition" 2002; Edwin Walker, "Mission Structures and Management Principles for the 21st Century" 2002;.

Chavannes Jeune, interview by author, tape recording, 5 November 2002)

While progress has been made in fulfilling our Messiah's intent for His Great Commission, if the above issues are not addressed appropriately and diligently, serious consequences could follow. Like a "sleeping giant," the Haitian Church would endanger its potential and miss the opportunity to make an everlasting impact in world evangelization as its contribution to the fulfillment of the Great Commission. Hence, Haitian believers would be eternally accountable to the Lord for misusing such wonderful opportunities. This would particularly be true in places where the host country might welcome fellow Haitians with God's eternal message of salvation while they at the same time may not welcome Western missionaries. Edwin Walker argued that "it is expected that by the year 2000 that 83% of the unreached people will be closed to Western missionaries but many of them will continue to be open to missionaries from some of the Two-Thirds World" (Edwin Walker, "Global Sharing," 2002). Moreover, testimonies from missionaries interviewed for this work abound and authenticate that affirmation (Fontus 2002; Firmin 2002; Joachin 2003; Desamour 2003; Deshommes 2003; Honore 2003; Amertil 2003; Eleazard 2003; Firmin 2003; Berthole 2003; Cadet 2003; Louis 2003; Destournel 2003).

Regarding the special and urgent opportunity available to Haitians to spread the gospel, one Haitian missionary shared this with the author:

> My integration in...(Africa) was easier because of my color. The people gave me a warm welcome. It would be an advantage for black people [such as Haitians] to participate in cross-cultural missions. Sometimes, when dealing with black people as missionaries, the tension diminished compared to white people, considered as colonizers. Lastly, it provides a good image for the host country because black people like them are involved in missions.

May God give new life and missionary passion to invigorate Haitian missions and stimulate the Haitian Church to the task entrusted to them by the Lord Jesus Christ toward the nations of the world!

CHAPTER 3:
METHODOLOGY OF
THE STUDY

Description of the Ministry Setting

The research concern revolved around what reasons helped explain a limited vision of the Great Commission in the Haitian Church. In the Introduction (Statement of the Problem), I stated the problem in light of the global vision of the missionary mandate. In chapter 1, I laid the foundation for a contemporary understanding of the theological and biblical basis of the Great Commission. In chapter 2, I identified at least five factors (from the literature reviewed) which contribute to the restrictive vision of the Great Commission in the Haitian Church:

(1)   Lack of adequate biblical teaching on missions

(2)   Inadequate applied theology and methodology

(3)   Deficient exposure to missions, both in seminary and in the church

(4)   Inadequate contextualization of the gospel,

(5)   Lack of challenge from missionaries and National Church pastors persuading Haitian believers to get involved in world missions

In this chapter, I focus on my questionnaire design. (See appendices 25 and 26 for copies of the questionnaire in English and French, respectively.)

After determining from the literature review and interviews with key people what the relevant issues were, I decided to develop a written survey to collect information that would make clear whether or not my assumptions regarding Haitian missions had any validity. My respondents included members of my congregation and other involved in or interested in Haitian missions.

The procedure for data collection was designed to help assess (by age group and gender) the congregants' cognitive, affective, and behavioral understanding of the missionary mandate. Thus I present in this section the subjects and population, the sampling method, the instrument, the procedures, and the analysis of data.

Subjects and Population

The Haitian population in the greater Chicago area at the time of the survey was estimated to be between 40,000 and 45,000 people. Among 18 churches serving the Haitian community in Chicago, twelve (12) were Evangelical and Pentecostal/ Charismatic, two (2) Seventh-Day Adventist, two (2) Roman Catholic, one (1) Body of Christ, and one (1) Jehovah's Witnesses.

The HMC, the congregation I pastor, is located in Evanston, Illinois, and serves primarily the Haitian community. That community is composed of Afro-Caribbeans and Afro-American Caribbeans. French and Creole are the primary languages spoken as well as English. Children coming from Haiti at an early stage or those born in the United States were sometimes limited in their understanding of French and Creole.

At the time of the survey, the HMC had an average attendance of 65 on Sunday. Sunday worship services at the HMC are generally held in French and Creole from 12:50 pm to 2:40 pm at the facilities of Evangelical Covenant Church of Evanston. English translation is provided for those who cannot understand French and Creole. During the week, a small group Bible study takes place on Tuesdays from 6:30 pm to 8:30 pm. The youth group study is done in English, and the adult study is done in French and Creole. Saturday prayer meetings are organized from 8:30 am to 10:45 am.

Description of the Ministry Study

SAMPLING METHOD

The HMC was designated as the sample. All the Evangelical and Pentecostal/Charismatic Haitian churches in Chicago were invited to participate in the data collection phase during a special service at the HMC. The actual attendance during that service represented the probability sample for that purpose. To gather probability data, the quantitative method embedded on a random sample was chosen. Some churchgoers did not attend when data collection was processed due to unforeseen circumstances such as work schedule, sickness, and so forth.

It is interesting to note at this point that based on the results of the study, it was determined that a similar study on an expanded basis would become valuable. First, it had the potential to provide an accurate assessment of the Haitians' cognitive, affective and behavioral understanding of the Great Commission in relation to their immediate environment. Second, we recognized that the questionnaire could be revised in order to make it fit the situational factors of various respondents, thus extending it for use as an interactive tool for other congregations and in other settings.

INSTRUMENTS

Since the Haitian population targeted was dispersed throughout the Chicago area and abroad, it became difficult to collect the opinion of the majority. Therefore, a survey was deemed the most feasible data collection instrument that could be used. It gave respondents a platform to voice their opinions. The questionnaire was constructed based on the operative supposition that what people were thinking could be known by what they say about a particular subject. In the questionnaire preparation process, I took into consideration the respondents' background, language of choice, and circumstances. In addition to making the content and the wording of the questions user-friendly, I considered the response format, the sequence of the questions, and the layout characteristics with the audience in mind. The content included multiple-choice questions, open-ended questions, and close-ended questions.

RESEARCH OBJECTIVES

In this section, I identified the areas in which information was needed. The kind of church that embraced a missionary vision and acted accordingly was defined. It was a church that knew what the Bible taught about the Great Commission, that was serious about evangelism and committed to missions.

INFORMATION NEED

In order to meet the objectives, specific information was needed. The questionnaires were formulated in such a way as to obtain that information. Thus, I constructed a list of information needs for that purpose. I believed that the information to be gained would be conducive to answering the objectives of the study. Consequently, each information need was related to specific questions on the questionnaire. For some needs, there were more than one related question; and, likewise, the answers to a single question sometimes could be seen as providing information relating to a number of different issues.

GATHERING INFORMATION

Information was gathered concerning three categories: The Holy Scriptures, the Great Commission, and the local church. Each category looked at three dimensions: cognitive (knowledge), affective (feelings), and behavioral (action). This structure was chosen to make it possible to develop appropriate teaching strategies to communicate the vision of the Great Commission to the Haitian Church.

DESIGN

The field research was conducted at HMC in three groups: adults, youth, and visiting churches. The actual method was a random selection. The method used for data collection was a self-administered questionnaire. Respondents filled out the questionnaire after a church service.

QUESTIONNAIRE COMPONENTS

Each questionnaire had a number, which was needed for control at the time of tabulation. On the anonymous questionnaire, the control number was added after the questionnaire was collected. Respondents received instruction on how to complete the questionnaire successfully. The instructions followed an introduction. Further directions were given accordingly whenever there was a need.

Demographic information was classified at the end of the questionnaire (questions 36 to 40). The response format for these questions was pre-coded so that respondents need only enter a single response to each question.

MAPPING OF THE QUESTIONNAIRE

In designing the questionnaire, a paragraph was carefully written in the introduction that appealed to the respondents to cooperate in an honest, objective way. Moreover, the questions that formed the body of the questionnaire were prepared in such a way that the necessary data would be obtained in order to answer the objectives of the study. For instance, question 2 was a direct, undisguised question: "To me Jesus' followers reported 5 versions of the Great Commission in the New Testament."

Question 10 was designed to find out if respondents could identify the responsibility attached to the Great Commission:

10. To me, the Great Commission was given:

    a) To the 12 disciples alone
    b) To all the disciples of Jesus Christ
    c) To every human being
    d) Don't know.

Questions 17 and 24 were designed to test the respondents' understanding (cognitive aspect) of the Great Commission, "For me the Great Commission is found…" and "In my opinion, the Great Commission means…"

Questions 3 and 23 were designed to test respondents' affective understanding of the missionary mandate: "I feel God gives to only a few people in the church the responsibility to share the gospel with people who have not heard it," and, "I feel that only the missionaries have the responsibility to go on the field."

Questions 21 and 33 were designed to assess the respondents' behavior regarding the missionary mandate: "If it fits my schedule, I would be open to a short-term, cross-cultural mission experience," and "Are you planning to go anywhere if God would call you as a missionary?"

TABULATION

All questionnaires were collected for central coding and tabulation.

PROCEDURES

In order to validate the questionnaire, a pre-test evaluation was administered with a group of Haitian pastors and laypeople on February 23, 2002. It took 9 to 13 minutes to fill out the questionnaire and proofread for clarity and potential discrepancy. The group gave valuable suggestions, and corrections were made to improve the sensitivity and clarity of the questions through interaction with the group.

Prior to giving the questionnaire to the congregants, announcements were made two weeks ahead of time for the congregation to make plans to stay after church service in order to help fill out the questionnaire. When the questionnaires were given out, those who attended church that day constituted our population. A group of six qualified people from the church were instructed prior to that event to take up the assignment and handle the data. Questionnaires were distributed only to those who were 8 years old or older.

The questionnaire was defined as follows:

Element:	Afro-Caribbean and Afro-American
	Caribbean congregants
Sampling Units:	Haitian Missionary Church
Extent:	Evanston, Illinois
Time:	May 12- 26, 2002

The sampling frame was the city map of the greater Chicago area.

The questionnaires were given and collected the same day between May 12 and 26, 2002. In order to guarantee the accuracy of the results, careful attention was given to how the data were obtained and recorded during the process.

The main objective for collecting the data was to evaluate the respondents' cognitive, affective, and behavioral understanding of the missionary mandate. The cognitive aspect of the study was designed to assess their knowledge of the Great Commission. The affective side attempted to uncover what they felt about the Great Commission. Finally, the behavioral aspect was to unearth what kind of behavior change (action) would occur in their lives with the application of the Great Commission.

In terms of historical validity of this study, between May 12 and May 26, 2002, during which the questionnaires were given and collected, nothing happened to the knowledge of the author to have nurtured a bias that would have nullified the data.

ANALYSIS OF DATA

When the questionnaires were filled out and collected in the church, the data were organized through figures and charts in order to make a valid test of the hypothesis. The nonparametric data were organized in table format. Then, the information collected was interpreted in order to validate or annul the assumptions detailed in the Introduction of the study (Basic Assumptions of the Study). The findings are presented in chapter 4, and my conclusions and recommendations on communicating a missionary vision according to the Great Commission are presented in chapter 5.

APPLICATION OF THE STUDY

I expect this study will be useful not only to the believer's personal walk with God but equally to the Haitian Church in general. The greatest hope is to see this research being used by God to accomplish at least the following:

(1) To communicate a sense of passion to Haitian believers in Haiti, to Haiti believers who live abroad, and particularly to members of the HMC in Evanston.

(2) To educate these believers in the following ways:

   a) The world-wide implications of the Great Commission as well as its local application.

   b) The responsibility of each Christian to share in the carrying out of the Great Commission as the Lord may lead: through prayer, encouragement, love, learning about and supporting mission endeavors, financial support, and open attitude as well as willingness to consider personal involvement before the Lord.

(3)   To provide a sense of life purpose and direction for the believers.

(4)   To foster also a sense of vision for the future.

(5)   To open doors in partnership with God in the salvation of mankind around the world.

(6)   To be and become believers who are committed to bringing a contribution to the fulfillment of the Great Commission.

RIPE NOW!

CHAPTER 4:
COLLECTING, ANALYZING, AND
INTERPRETING THE DATA

Collecting the Data

As discussed in chapter 3, the questionnaires were distributed at the HMC as scheduled. We distributed them in three different sessions: to the adults, the youth, and a gathering of 10 Haitian Evangelical and Pentecostal/Charismatic churches in Chicago. The questionnaire consisted of 42 questions that were primarily designed to collect the data for an assessment of the respondents' cognitive, affective, behavioral understanding of the missionary mandate. Out of 115 questionnaires distributed, 109 were returned completed from May 12 to 26, 2002. I promised to share the findings with respondents following the completion of the research.

Data Analysis

The data collected were analyzed in six different sections: General Observation, Demographic, Cognitive, Affective, Behavioral, and Supplementary Analysis.

GENERAL OBSERVATION

This section is designed to present a general overview of the data analysis. It is divided into three categories: the summary of the questions, the number of questions, and the items. All data were measured in percentages except in question 34. The results are presented in appendix 8.

DEMOGRAPHIC

This section covered the demographic part of the analysis.

Conversion Group
(Question 35: Are you a Christian?)

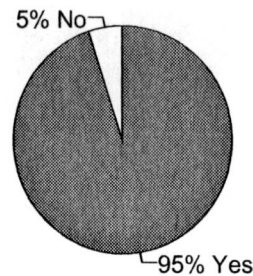

5% No

95% Yes

FIG. 2. CONVERSION CATEGORY

In figure 2, 95 percent of the respondents said they were Christians compared to 5 percent who answered negatively.

Length of Time Living in America
(Question 36)

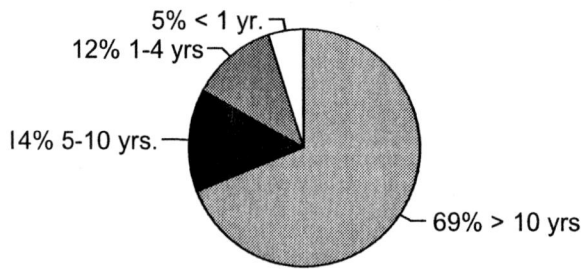

5% < 1 yr.

12% 1-4 yrs

14% 5-10 yrs.

69% > 10 yrs.

FIG. 3. LENGTH OF TIME LIVING IN AMERICA

In figure 3, 5 percent of the respondents recorded living in America for less than a year, 12 percent stated between 1 and 4 years, 14 percent affirmed between 5 and 10 years, and 69 percent said they had lived in America for more than 10 years.

Age Group Demographics
(Question 37)

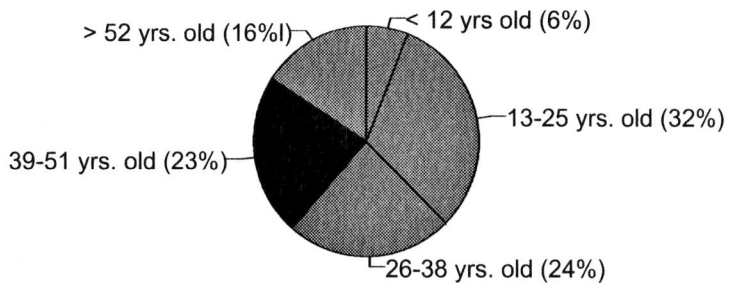

FIG. 4. AGE GROUPS OF THE RESPONDENTS

In figure 4, 6 percent of the respondents said they were less than 12 years of age, 32 percent were between 13 and 25 years old, 24 percent were between 26 and 38 years old, 23 percent were between 39 and 51 years old, and 16 percent were at least 52 years old. It was worth noting that 56 percent of the respondents were between 13 and 38 years of age, representing the second and third age groups combined together.

Gender Group
(Question 38)

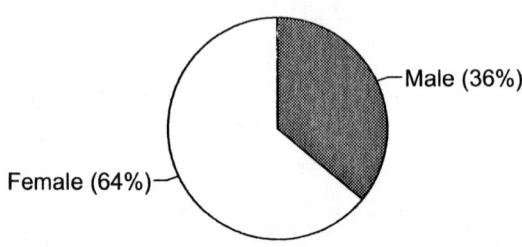

FIG. 5. GENDER CATEGORY

In figure 5, 36 percent of the respondents were male compared to 64 percent female.

Length of Time as a Christian
(Question 39)

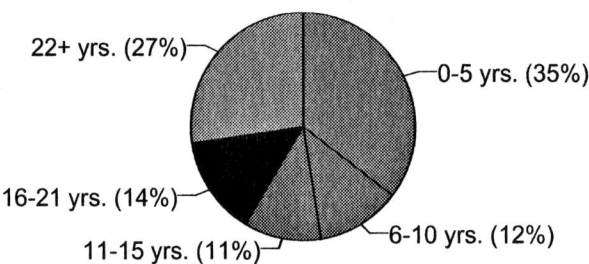

FIG. 6. LENGTH OF TIME THE RESPONDENTS HAVE BEEN CHRISTIANS

In figure 6, 35 percent of the respondents have been Christian for between 0-5 years, 12 percent between 6 and 10 years, 11 percent between 11 and 15 years, 14 percent between 16 and 21 years, and 27 percent have been Christians for 22 years or more.

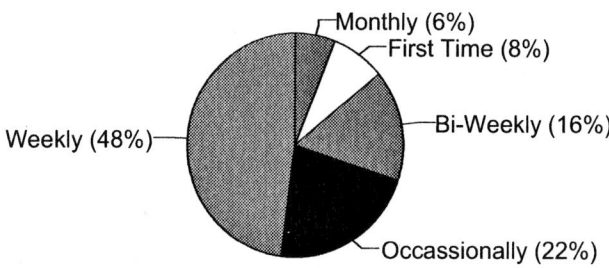

FIG. 7. ATTENDANCE CATEGORY

In figure 7, 48 percent of the respondents attended church weekly, 6 percent monthly, 8 percent for the first time, 16 percent bi-weekly, and 22 percent occasionally.

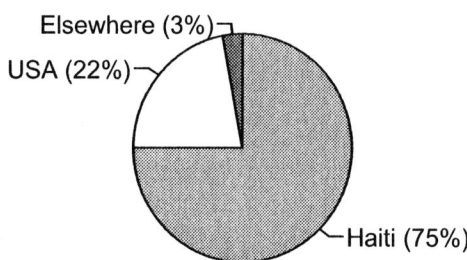

FIG. 8. BIRTH PLACE CATEGORY

In figure 8, 75 percent of the respondents were born in Haiti, 22 percent in the USA, and 3 percent elsewhere.

Church Visitors and Home Church
(Question 42)

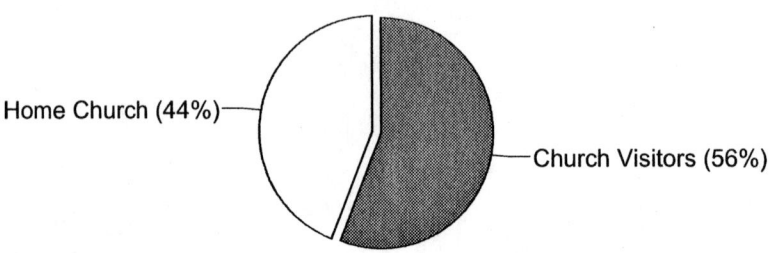

Home Church (44%)

Church Visitors (56%)

FIG. 9. VISITING CHURCH AND HOME CHURCH CATEGORIES

In figure 9, 56 percent claimed to be visitors and 44 percent were assumed to belong to the home church (HMC).

Language Comfortability

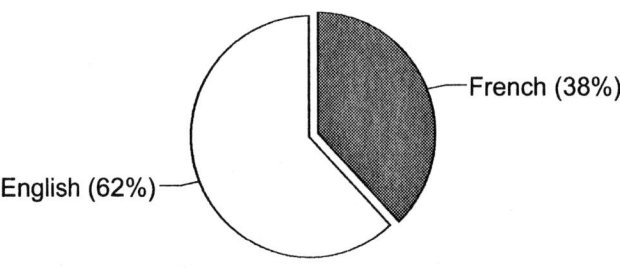

French (38%)

English (62%)

FIG. 10. DEGREE OF COMFORT IN THE LANGUAGE

In figure 10, 62 percent of the respondents felt comfortable answering the questionnaire in English whereas 38 percent answered in French.

In summary, this section provided a broader understanding of the demographic situation of the respondents. Among 75 percent of the respondents born in Haiti, 46 percent were females and 41 percent were believers. This was likely to show that the majority of believing females in the Haitian Church were categorically immigrants from Haiti.

COGNITIVE

In this section, the data were analyzed to determine the cognitive understanding of the respondents in relation to the Great Commission.

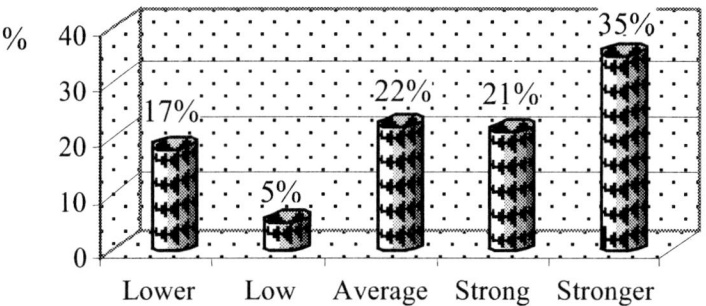

Knowledge of the Great Commission
(Question 1)

FIG. 11. KNOWLEDGE OF THE MISSIONARY MANDATE

In figure 11, 17 percent of the respondents indicated a "lower" understanding of the Great Commission, 5 percent were "low," 22 percent were "average," 21 percent were "strong," and 35 percent were "stronger." When combined, answers of "strong" and "stronger reached a total of 56 percent.

5 Versions of the Great Commission?
(Question 2)

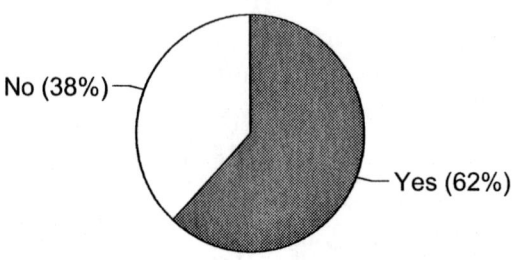

FIG. 12. VERSIONS OF THE GREAT COMMISSION CATEGORY

In figure 12, 62 percent of the respondents affirmed a positive knowledge of the Great Commission compared to 38 percent who thought otherwise.

Great Commission Understanding

Question 10: Who Is Responsible?

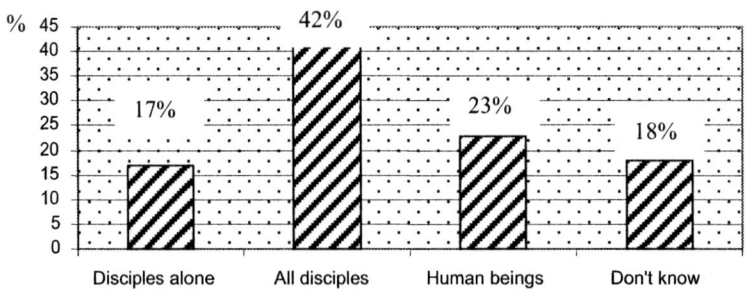

FIG. 13. GREAT COMMISSION GROUP

In figure 13, 17 percent of the respondents believed that the Great Commission was given to the disciples alone, 42 percent applied it for all disciples, 23 percent believed it was given to human beings, and 18 percent did not know to whom it was given.

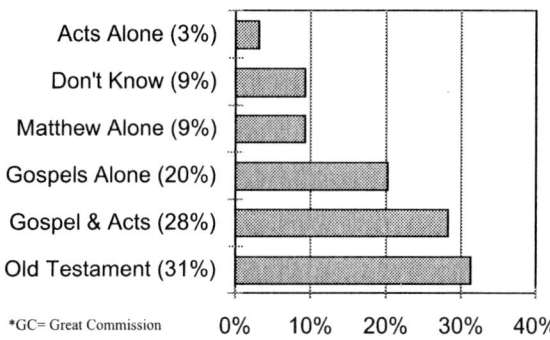

Great Commission Assessment
Question 17: Where is the GC* found?

FIG. 14. GREAT COMMISSION LOCATION

In figure 14, 3 percent of respondents believed the Great Commission could be found in Acts alone, 9 percent did not know where to find the Great Commission, 9 percent thought it was in Matthew alone, 20 percent believed it was found in the Gospels alone, 28 percent believed it was in the Gospels and Acts, and 31 percent assumed it was in the Old Testament.

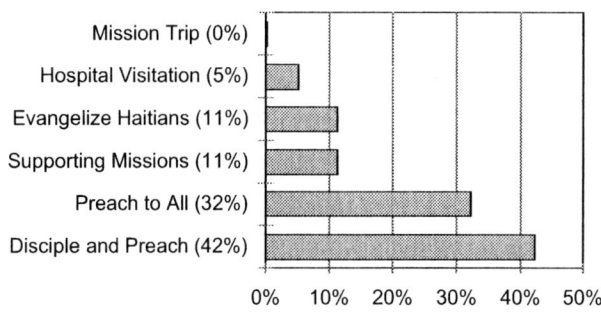

Meaning of Great Commission
Question 24

FIG. 15. SIGNIFICANCE OF THE GREAT COMMISSION

In figure 15, 5 percent took the Great Commission to mean "hospital visitation," 11 percent to mean "supporting missionaries if I cannot go," 11 percent believed the Great Commission to mean "evangelize specially the Haitians," 32 percent believed it meant to "preach the gospel to Haitians and all the people on earth," and 42 percent thought it meant to "preach the gospel to all nations and make disciples."

In summary, the cognitive analysis displayed the respondents' knowledge of the Great Commission. In general, between 35 to 62 percent of congregants claimed to have a good cognitive understanding of the missionary mandate. However, the highest score (31 percent) in figure 14 indicated that congregants believed to find the Great Commission in the Old Testament.

AFFECTIVE

In this section the data were analyzed to determine the affective understanding of the respondents in relation to the Great Commission.

Responsibility to Share the Gospel

Question 3: Only a few people are responsible

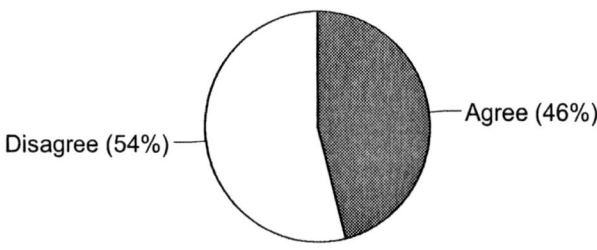

FIG. 16. BELIEVERS' RESPONSIBILITY TO SHARE THE GOSPEL

In figure 16, 46 percent of the respondents felt that God gave to a few people in the Church the responsibility to share the gospel with those who have not heard it; whereas, 54 percent believed otherwise.

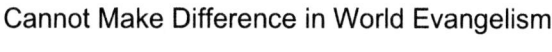

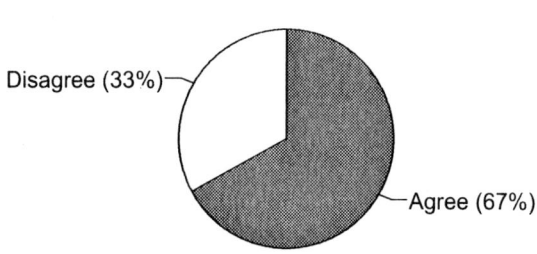

FIG. 17. "I CAN'T MAKE A DIFFERENCE IN WORLD EVANGELIZATION"

In figure 17, 67 percent of respondents felt they could not make any difference in world evangelization; whereas, 33 percent thought they could. In other words, 2 out of 3 respondents do not feel they can make a difference.

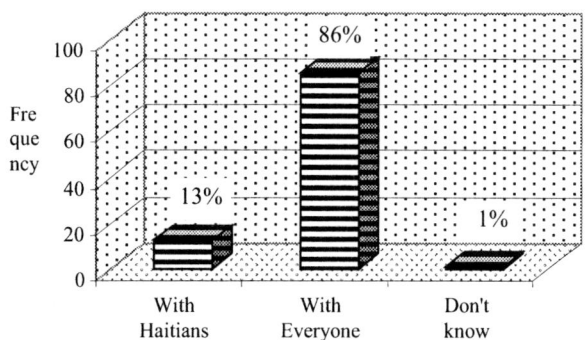

FIG. 18. RESPONDENTS' ASSESSMENT OF CHURCH RESPONSIBILITY

In figure 18, 13 percent of the respondents felt that the Church needed to share the gospel with Haitians, 86 percent felt that the church needed to share the gospel with everyone, and 1 percent did not know.

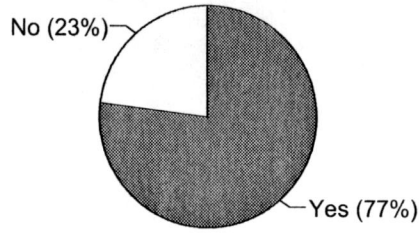

FIG. 19. AFFECTIVE UNDERSTANDING OF THE GREAT COMMISSION

In figure 19, 77 percent of respondents felt what they learned in church contributed to understanding the Great Commission and 23 percent disagreed with that assessment.

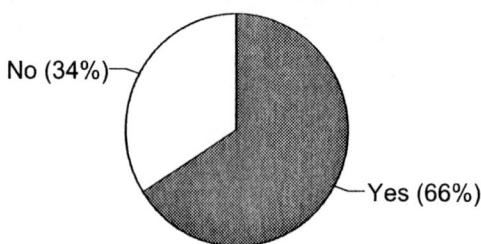

FIG. 20. RESPONDENTS' ASSESSMENT OF MISSIONARIES' RESPONSIBILITY

In figure 20, 66 percent felt that only missionaries have the responsibility to go to foreign fields; whereas, 34 percent did not share that idea. In fact 2 out of 3 the respondents felt that missionaries were the ones responsible to go to the fields.

In summary, the affective analysis showed in general that 87 the respondents out of 100 (or approximately 9 out of 10) felt it was the responsibility of the Church to share the gospel with everyone. In contrast, 46 percent said they did not feel that everyone in the Church had that responsibility. Sixty-nine (69) percent changed their opinion to affirm that missions work was the responsibility of every church, including theirs. Similarly, 74 percent felt that missions work was also the responsibility of every believer including themselves. It appeared that the respondents were not consistent at this level and thus provided conflicting statements. Finally, 66 percent of respondents (2 congregants out of 3) felt that it was not their responsibility to go to the missions fields. Instead, they believed the missionaries were responsible for that duty.

BEHAVIORAL

In this section, the data were analyzed to determine the behavioral understanding of the respondents in relation to the Great Commission.

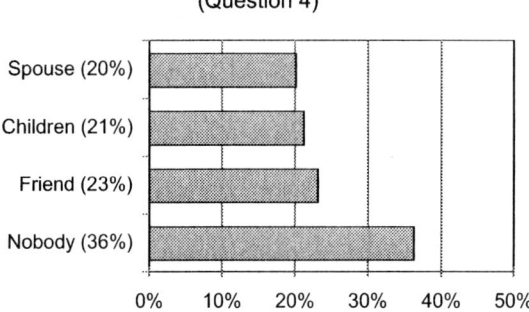

If I Could Not Go, I Would Send...

(Question 4)

FIG. 21. SUBSTITUTION TO GOD'S CALLING

In figure 21, 20 percent of the respondents affirmed that if they could not go on a mission, they would send their spouses; 21 percent would send their children; 23 percent would send their best friends, and 36 percent would send none.

Choice of Countries to Serve as a Missionary

Question 8

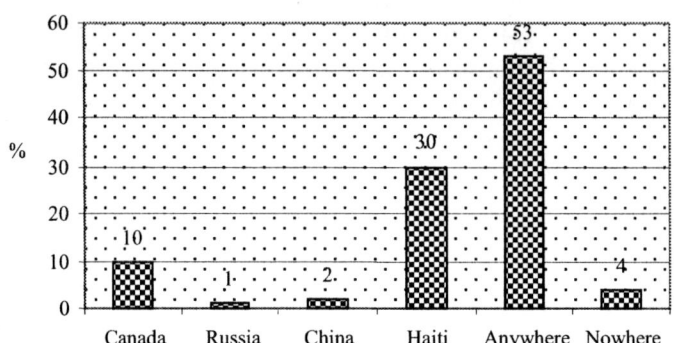

FIG. 22. PLACES OF PREFERENCE TO SERVE AS A MISSIONARY

In figure 22, 10 percent of the respondents asserted if God would call them as a missionary, they would go to Canada, 1 percent would go to Russia, 2 percent would go to China, 30 percent would go to Haiti, 53 percent stressed they would go anywhere, and 4 percent would go nowhere.

Willingness to Give Up
(Question 14)

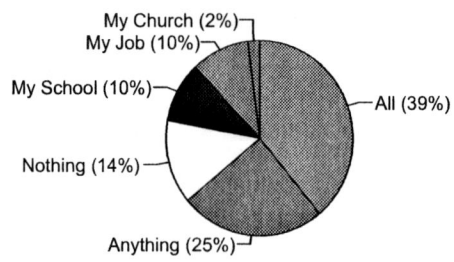

FIG. 23. RESPONSE TO GOD'S CALLING

In figure 23, 2 percent of respondents said they would relinquish their church if God would call them as a missionary, 10 percent affirmed they would resign from their jobs, 10 percent would abandon their schools, 14 percent would hand over anything if they were called, 25 percent would give up "anything," and 39 percent would surrender "all." The grouping of "anything" and "all" together represented 64 percent of the respondents.

Obstacles to Evangelism

Q 19: Reaching the lost is important, but I can't see myself doing it.

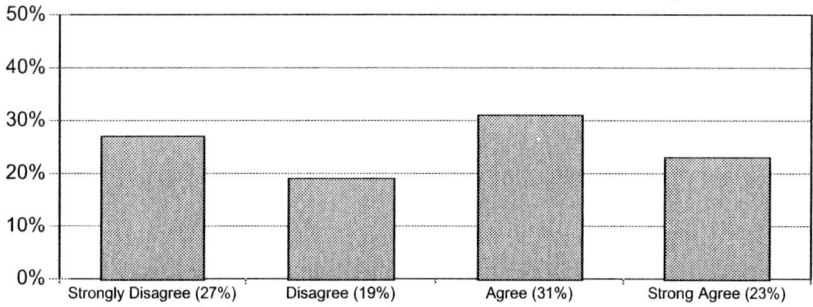

FIG. 24. HINDRANCES TO EVANGELISM

In figure 24, 27 percent of respondents stated that they strongly disagreed with the statement that they would not reach the lost people for Christ though it was important. Nineteen (19) percent somewhat disagreed with that statement, 31 percent agreed, and 23 percent strongly agreed. Combined together, those who agreed with the statement (that they would not reach the lost) represented 54 percent of the respondents.

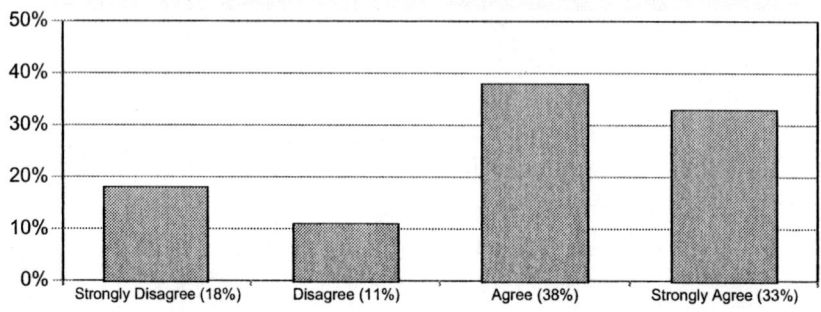

Openness to Cross-Cultural Missions

Q 21: If it fits my schedule, I would be open to short-term, cross-cultural missions

FIG. 25. AVAILABILITY TO CROSS-CULTURAL MISSIONS

In figure 25, 18 percent of the respondents strongly disagreed that they would be open to short-term missions experience even when it would fit their schedule; 11 percent somewhat disagreed; 38 percent agreed, and 33 percent strongly agreed. Linked together, those who would make themselves available represented 71 percent of respondents.

Willingness to Obey GC*
(Question 29: "No matter the cost")

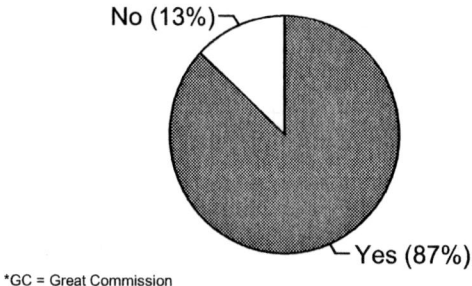

*GC = Great Commission

FIG. 26. COMPLIANCE TO THE GREAT COMMISSION

In figure 26, 87 percent of respondents said they were willing to obey the Great Commission no matter the cost; whereas, 13 percent were not ready to do so.

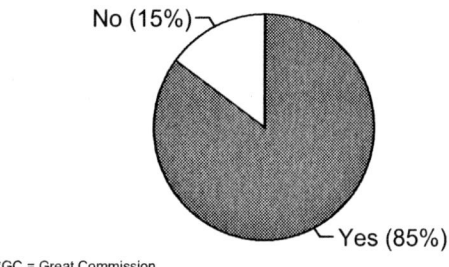

Willingness to Obey GC*
(Question 29: "Would go anywhere")

No (15%)

Yes (85%)

*GC = Great Commission

FIG. 27. RESPONDENT'S DECISION TO GOD'S CALL

In figure 27, 85 percent of the respondents were planning to go anywhere if God would call them as missionaries as opposed to 15 percent who did not share the same opinion.

In summary, the behavioral analysis section showed that 87 percent of the respondents said they were willing to obey the Great Commission at any cost. Likewise, 85 percent were willing to go anywhere if called by God as a missionary. However, 37 percent of the respondents affirmed if they could not go, they would send no one. Likewise, 54 percent agreed that reaching the lost for Christ was important, but they couldn't see themselves doing it. Finally, 71 percent agreed that only if it did fit their schedule they would be open to short-term, cross-cultural experience.

SUPPLEMENTARY ANALYSIS

In this section, five items were considered for data analysis: assumptions, male and female perspectives, age group's point of view, visiting church perspective compared to home church perspectives, and motivational factors.

Assumptions

The general view of data analysis in appendix 8 showed that 68 percent of all the respondents believed that missions was equated to hospital visitation. Likewise, 55 percent of respondents in age group 13-25, 70 percent of respondents in age group 26-38, 60 percent of respondents in age group 39-51 and 63 percent of respondents in age group 51 and over shared the same opinion. Similarly, 65 percent of females and 56 percent of males supported the same belief. Finally, 80 percent of respondents from the visiting churches compared to 84 percent of respondent of the home church held the same view. On the other hand, 63 percent of respondents believed that missions was helping the poor. Likewise, 70 percent of respondents believed that missions was sharing the gospel with prisoners in jail. Moreover, 64 percent of age group 13-25, 61 percent of age group 25-38, 40 percent of age group 39-51, and 69 percent of age group 52 and over maintained the same opinion. Furthermore, 67 percent of females and 59 percent of males affirmed the same belief. Finally, 72 percent of visiting churches and 58 percent of the home church shared the same view.

In summary, respondents in all age groups, females and males as well as visiting churches and the home church appeared to equate missions with hospital visitation, helping the poor, and sharing the gospel with prisoners in jail.

Male and Female Perspectives

On a cognitive level, 53 percent of females claimed to have a greater knowledge of the Great Commission compared to 46 percent of males.

On an affective level, 61 percent of females compared to 46 percent of males felt that God gave to only a few people in the church the responsibility to share the gospel with people who have not heard it. Moreover, 64 percent of females felt that they were at ease sharing their faith with others while 49 percent of males felt otherwise. In addition, 89 percent of females felt that their church needed to share the gospel compared to 84 percent of males. Finally, 64 percent of females felt what they learned in their church helped them understand the Great Commission compared to 49 percent of males.

On a behavioral level, 45 percent of females believed that reaching the lost for Christ was important, but they couldn't see themselves doing it, compared to 35 percent of males. Likewise, 50 percent of females stated that the way they live now reflects the Great Commission in comparison to 65 percent of males.

In summary, females seemed to have a different understanding of the Great Commission than males regardless of the categories under consideration (cognitive, affective, and behavioral).

Age Group's Point of View

Comparison was made between age group 13-25 and higher groups for analysis. On a cognitive level, 27 percent of age group 13-25 stated that they did not know where the Great Commission was found; whereas, 25 percent of group 26-38 affirmed the same thing, 9 percent of age group 39-51 shared the same opinion, and 6 percent of age group 52 and over held the same view.

On an affective level, 82 percent of age group 13-25 did not feel that God gave to only a few people in the church the responsibility to share the gospel with those who have not heard it. Likewise 58 percent of age group 26-38 supported that idea, 35 percent of age group 39-51 held the same opinion, and 25 percent of age group 52 and over maintained the same view.

On a behavioral level, 42 percent of age group 13-25 believed that they can't see themselves making any difference in the huge task of world evangelization; whereas, 38 percent of age group 26-38 responded the same way, 30 percent of age group 39-51 had the same understanding, and 6 percent of age group 52 and over agreed with that statement. Likewise, 82 percent of age group 13 25 said they were willing to obey the Great Commission no matter the cost, while 71 percent of age group 26-38 agreed with that, 78 percent of age group 39-51 supported that claim, and 44 percent of age group 52 and over had no reservation. Similarly, 36 percent of age group 13-25 said they would give up anything if God would call them as a missionary, compared to 29 percent of age group 26-38 who would do the same. Twenty-two (22) percent of age group 39-51 shared the same idea, and in age group 52 and over, none would give up anything, whether God would call them as a missionary or not. Along the same lines, 55 percent of age group 13-25 believed that reaching the lost for Christ was important, but they could not see themselves doing it; whereas, 46 percent of age group 26-38 agreed with that statement, 26 percent of age group 39-51 shared the same opinion, and 31 percent of age group 52 and over supported that idea. In addition, 33 percent of age group 13-25 was thinking that the way they live now reflects the mandate of the Great Commission, 63 percent of age group 26-38 believed the same thing, 65 percent of age group 39-51 confirmed that statement, and 94 percent age group 52 and over supported that same idea. Finally, 76 percent of age group 13-25 agreed that only if it did fit their schedule they would be open to short-term, cross-cultural mission experience while 67 percent of age group 26-38 stated the same thing, 57 percent of age group 39-51 understood it that way as well, and 50 percent of age group 52 and over argued in favor of it.

In summary, the respondents in age group 13-25 appeared to show a better understanding overall than the rest of the groups (26-38, 39-51, 52 and over) in all three categories (cognitive, affective, behavioral).

Visiting Church Perspectives Compared to Home Church Perspectives

In this section, comparison was made between the visiting churches and the home church in Evanston (HMC).

On a cognitive level, 47 percent of the respondents of the visiting churches claimed that the Great Commission was given to all disciples of Jesus Christ compared to 36 percent of the respondents of the home church. However, 26 percent of the respondents of the visiting churches believed that the Great Commission was found in the Gospel and Acts compared to 32 percent of the respondents of the home church who were of the same opinion.

On an affective level, 52 percent of the respondents from visiting churches felt that God only gave to a few people in the church the responsibility to share the gospel with those who have not heard it compared to 55 percent of the respondents of the home church. Likewise, 58 percent of respondents of visiting churches supported the idea that only missionaries have a responsibility to go the fields, compared to 71 percent in the respondents of home church.

On a behavioral level, 58 percent of respondents of visiting churches believed they would go anywhere if God would call them as missionaries compared to 49 percent of the respondents of the home church. Likewise, 21 percent of the respondents of visiting churches believed that reaching lost people for Christ was important but they could not see themselves doing. In comparison, 38 percent of the respondents of the home church believed the same. However, 24 percent of respondents of the visiting churches said they would give up nothing if called by God as missionaries compared to 11 percent of respondents of the home church.

In summary, the respondents in the churches visited and in the home church have presented both strengths and weaknesses depending on the categories under consideration.

Motivational Factors

Congregants who responded to question 34 provided helpful information that can served as a catalyst for communicating a missionary vision to the Haitian Church.

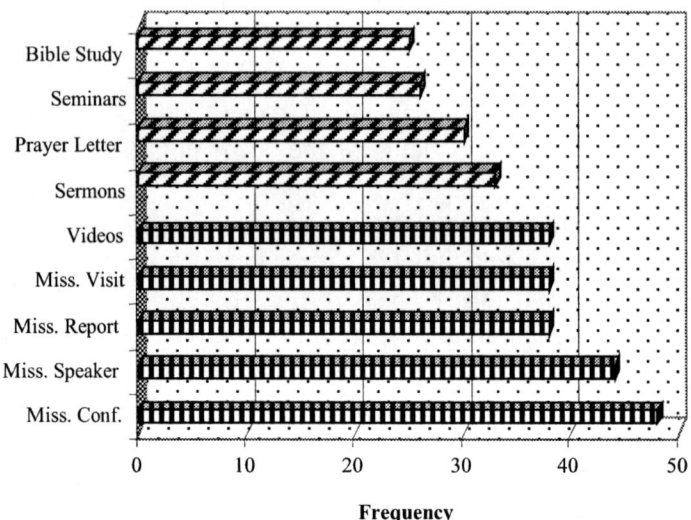

FIG. 28. MOTIVATIONAL ELEMENTS

As shown in figure 28, the general view of data analysis in appendix 8 showed four factors to be less motivating: Sermons (33), Prayer Letter (30), Bible Study (27), Seminars (26). The respondents have identified five key motivating factors in units rather than in percentage that can be helpful: missions conference (48 respondents), missionary speakers (44 respondents), missions report (38 respondents), missionary visits (38 respondents), and videos (38 respondents).

In conclusion, the cognitive, affective, behavioral, and supplementary section provided another picture of the data analysis not only between females and males, but in comparison of age group 13-25 to the higher groups as well as visiting churches compared to the home church. The results had the tendency to show particular aspects that would have been otherwise difficult to notice. Suffice it to say at this point that both females and age group 13-25 have the highest score in most cases compared to their counterparts. Therefore, they may have the potential to influence to a great deal the outcome of this analysis and future decisions that could be made.

Interpreting the Data

In this section, the data were interpreted in four categories: cognitive, affective, behavioral, and supplementary interpretation.

COGNITIVE

The purpose of this section was to interpret the data relating to the cognitive understanding of respondents.

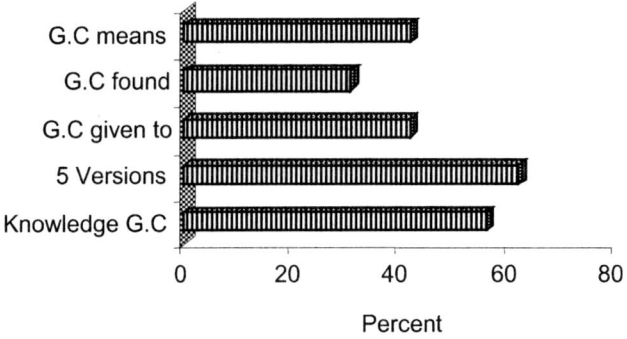

Cognitive Comparison of the Great Commission

FIG. 29. COMPARISON OF THE GREAT COMMISSION

In figure 29, the highest scores relating to the cognitive understanding of the Great Commission were compared for evaluation purposes. It came out that the highest score for the first three answers above (GC means, GC found, GC given to) were below 50 percent. These items were the ones which can be used to assess an accurate understanding of respondents' knowledge of the Great Commission. The remaining two that reached above 50 percent may be perceived to be more related to personal opinion.

In summary, it was argued that the respondents assumed to know what the Great Commission was all about. Nonetheless, their answers failed to confirm that they did indeed have an accurate knowledge of the missionary mandate. This finding has the tendency to reflect the cultural aspect of respondents, who often overestimated their understanding of a particular subject.

AFFECTIVE

The above data analysis seemed to show that 87 respondents out of 100 (or approximately 9 out of 10) argued that the burden of sharing the gospel worldwide has fallen on the local church. In addition, 69 percent of respondents were still thinking that missions was the responsibility of the church, including theirs. Even though 92 percent felt that they were at ease sharing their faith with others, when it came to their involvement in world evangelization, they failed to provide real evidence of personal responsibility. For instance, 67 percent cannot see themselves making any difference in world evangelization. Likewise, 46 percent said they did not feel that everyone in the church had that responsibility, compared to 87 respondents out of 100 (or roughly 9 out of 10) who said they would go anywhere if God called them as missionary. Conversely, 2 people out of 3 (66 percent) felt the task of being involved in the mission fields remained the responsibility of missionaries rather than being their own responsibility.

In summary, it appeared that the respondents did not feel ready to take on personal responsibility for world evangelization. Rather, they saw the task as one being done by the church or the missionary. At the same time, most of them felt that the burden of sharing the gospel worldwide has fallen on the church, and felt at ease sharing their faith with others. Therefore, the respondents showed a great deal of inconsistency in their affective understanding of the Great Commission.

BEHAVIORAL

Earlier data analysis showed that 87 percent of respondents appeared to claim they were willing to obey the Great Commission at any cost. Likewise, 77 percent said that what they learned from their church contributed to their understanding of the Great Commission. Similarly, 74 percent of respondents asserted that missions was the responsibility of every believer including themselves. Seventy-one (71) percent of respondents agreed that they would be open to cross-cultural missions experience even if it fitted their schedule. Similarly, 54 percent argued in favor of reaching the lost for Christ, but they saw others more fitting to fulfill that task than themselves. In addition, 36 percent of the respondents believed that if they could not respond to God's call as a missionary, they would send no one regardless of circumstances. Meanwhile, 77 respondents out of 100 (or approximately 7 out of 10) said they understood the missionary mandate while at the same time the same number of people (7 out of 10) argued that their participation in the fulfillment of the Great Commission was contingent upon their schedule. In contrast, 87 respondents out of 100 (or roughly 9 out of 10) claimed their willingness to obey the Great Commission.

In summary, the above data showed incoherence in the attitude of respondents regarding their potential involvement in the missionary mandate. This picture had the tendency to show realistically how the respondents intended to act based on their knowledge of the Great Commission.

SUPPLEMENTARY INTERPRETATION

In this section, five items were considered for interpretation: assumptions, male and female perspectives, age group's point of view, visiting church perspectives compared to home church perspectives, and motivational factors.

Assumptions

Earlier analysis demonstrated that more than 62 percent of the respondents seemed to equate missions with hospital visitation, helping the poor, and sharing the gospel with prisoners in jail. It was believed that both caregiving and local evangelism can be incorporated into missionary work. Nevertheless, to see all three of these activities as equivalent to missions might mislead people as the true nature of missions and thus limit their perspective.

Male and Female Perspectives

In comparing female and male understanding of the missionary mandate, females had a more favorable assessment of their understanding of the Great Commission compared to the males' assessment of their own understanding. At the same time, more females had the tendency to limit missions to a local milieu compared to males. A limited view of missions could also be seen in the affective area as well. For instance, 61 percent of females compared to 46 percent of males felt that God gave to only a few people in the church the responsibility to share the gospel with people who have not heard it. On a behavioral level, more females were inclined to be affected than males because of their greater percentage (45 percent of females believed that reaching lost people for Christ was important, but they couldn't see themselves doing it compared to 35 percent of males). On the other hand, when it came to a lifestyle that reflected the Great Commission, male claims overshadowed those of females in that capacity (65 over 50 percent).

Perspectives by Age group

In age group comparison, it revealed that the age group 13-25 appeared to perform better than the older age groups. For instance, age group 13-25 had a greater percentage (27 percent) than the rest (respectively 25, 9, and 6 percent) when it came to making an assessment of their cognitive understanding of the missionary mandate. This trend did not change when it came to the affective level. In fact, age group 13-25 continued to perform better. For example, the age group 13-25 outdid the other groups in the behavioral level in relation to their obedience to the Great Commission and in response to God's call to be a missionary. For instance, 82 percent of age group 13-25 was willing to obey the Great Commission at any cost in comparison to 71 percent of age group 26-38, 78 percent of age group 39-51, and 44 percent of age group 52 and over. Furthermore, 36 percent of age group 13-25 was willing to give up anything if God would call them as missionaries compared to 29 percent of age group 26-38, 22 percent of age group 39-51, and none in age group 52 and over.

On the other hand, the age group 13-25 performance showed some difficulty when it came to world evangelization. For instance, 55 percent of age group 13-25 believed that reaching lost people for Christ was important, but they could not see themselves doing it, compared to 46 percent age group 26-38, 26 percent of age group 39-51, and 31 percent of age group 52 and over. Likewise, 42 percent of age group 13-25 could not see themselves making any difference in the huge task of world evangelization, compared to 38 percent of age group 26-38, 30 percent of age group 39-51, and 6 percent of age group 52 and over. Finally, 76 percent of age group 13-25 agreed that only if it did fit their schedule they would be open to a short-term, cross-cultural mission experience, compared to 67 percent of age group 26-38, 57 percent of age group 39-51, and 50 percent of age group 52 and over. Equally, 82 percent of the respondents in age group 13-25 felt that God gave to only a few people in the church the responsibility to share the gospel with those who have not heard it, in comparison to 58 percent for age group 26-38, 35 percent for age group 39-51, and 25 percent for age group 52 and over. Thus, it appears that compared to the other age groups, the 13-25 age group had more difficulty getting involved in world evangelization. On the other hand, age group 52 and over showed some discrepancy when it came to their attitude towards the Great Commission. For instance, 94 percent claimed that their lifestyle reflected the mandate of the Great Commission. At the same time, none was willing to give up anything to respond to God's call to be a missionary.

In summary, the age group 13-25 showed a greater cognitive, affective, and behavioral understanding of the Great Commission than the other groups surveyed.

Visiting Church Compared to Home Church
Perspectives

In this section, a comparison between the visiting churches and the home church in Evanston (HMC) did not show great nuances at any level whether cognitive, affective, or behavioral. However, it appeared that both the visiting churches and the home church confirmed the assumptions that missions was equated to hospital visitation and sharing the gospel to prisoners in jail (80 compared to 84 percent). Finally, respondents from both sides missed an opportunity to affirm an accurate view of the missionary mandate.

In summary, visiting and home churches showed strengths and weaknesses in their understanding of the Great Commission.

Motivational Factors

All five key motivational factors have to do with physical presence of missionaries. In contrast, the previous four elements did not deal with missionaries themselves. It was assumed that the respondents might be more inclined to hear missionaries who have been on the field rather than to have a lecture or a sermon about missions from those who did not go to the mission fields. Furthermore, the presence of missionaries gives congregants an opportunity to interact with them on various issues or to receive them at home for fellowship. While sermons on missions have a particular place in the communication process, nonetheless, that technique does not appear to be the primary avenue or the most effective way to achieve that purpose according to the respondents.

Conclusion

The findings of this survey appeared to show that the respondents failed to confirm an accurate knowledge of the Great Commission. Likewise, their feelings about the missionary mandate did not seem to be coherent throughout. In general, respondents seemed reluctant when it comes to participating fully in the fulfillment of the Great Commission.

The respondents confirmed the assumption that missions was a misunderstood concept in the Haitian Church in general. The survey showed that some of them believed that missions was equivalent to hospital visitation while others understood it as helping the poor and sharing the gospel with prisoners in jail. Nonetheless, the younger generation (13-25) age group appeared to have a better understanding of the Great Commission than the previous generations (26-51 and over). Similarly, females emerged with a different perspective of the missionary mandate than males. Finally, when Jesus' model of the missionary mandate (in chapter 1) was compared to the respondents understanding of the Great Commission, there were differences between the two. In the next chapter, I have suggested appropriate steps to help the Haitian Church more fully embrace the Great Commission in its global perspective.

CHAPTER 5:
SUMMARY, CONCLUSIONS, RECOMMENDATIONS

Summary

My study of the problem of the apparent limited vision of the Great Commission within the Haitian Missionary Church led me to investigate the theological basis of the research (chapter 1). What I found in the Scriptures led me to an unmistakable global vision of the missionary mandate. That all-inclusive vision was based on Jesus' approach to His own mission; His approach to calling and equipping His disciples; and His instructions to His followers both before and after His resurrection. Although there are different versions of the Great Commission recorded in the New Testament, my studies showed that choice of one version over another, whether in teaching or in practice, can lead to misunderstanding. I discovered Jesus' approach to the Great Commission was to put identical emphasis on evangelism and disciple-making, with equal emphasis on geographical structure for carrying it out at home, regionally, and globally. His command appears to be thus formulated to ensure the gospel message is shared with people from all ethnic groups, countries, and religions.

As I reviewed the literature, I found that the pioneers of missions in Haiti had used an approach inconsistent with Jesus' model. Acts 1:8 appeared to be the text missionaries favored in the transfer of their missionary vision, with the result that Haitians reached out primarily to their own people. While it appears there has been a resurgence of mission work in the past century, a lot of work remains yet to be done.

My literature reviewed revealed that among the factors contributing to the adoption of a restrictive view of the Great Commission in the Haitian Church, five emerged as the most likely causes:

(1) Lack of adequate biblical teaching on missions

(2) Poorly applied theology and methodology

(3) Scanty exposure to missions both in seminaries and in the church

(4) Inadequate contextualization of the gospel

(5) Lack of challenge from missionaries and National Church pastors to encourage believers to get involved in world missions

The perception of the obstacles led me to design the procedures outlined in chapter 3 in order to assess my congregants' understanding of the Great Commission. The data were collected from the HMC and nine other Evangelical and Pentecostal/ Charismatic Haitian churches in Chicago.

I analyzed the data collected and came to many fascinating conclusions. Was there a difference of understanding between males and females or between adults and younger generations? The findings of this survey as explained in chapter 4 revealed that males have a different understanding of the Great Commission than that of females. Likewise, the younger generation held views generally different from those of the older generation. For many, the Great Commission was particularly related to many efforts combined to reaching out predominantly to Haitians in their own community. For some congregants, missions was equated to hospital visitation. For others, missions meant helping the poor or sharing the gospel with prisoners in jail.

This study convinced me more than ever that the global vision of the Great Commission is intended to compel the Church of Jesus Christ to reach other ethnic groups in the world. It is true that home is the point of departure, but the National Church needs to extend its outreach beyond its own country as well. Comparing Jesus' model of the missionary mandate (in chapter 1) with the respondents' understanding of the Great Commission reveals that Haitians have a limited vision of the Great Commission.

Finally in this chapter, I present conclusions and recommendations that I believe will be of help in communicating the missionary vision to the Haitian Church.

Conclusions

My analysis and interpretation (chapter 4) confirmed my hypotheses regarding the respondents' attitude towards the missionary mandate. Seventy-seven (77) percent of the respondents felt what they learned from their church helped them understand the Great Commission. Their understanding of the missionary mandate carried a three-fold implication. First, it became clear that the congregation had embraced the limited vision of the Great Commission that had been transferred to the Haitian leaders, both in teaching and practice, for decades. Second, earlier analysis (chapter 4) showed the respondents failed to demonstrate an accurate knowledge of the Great Commission according to the four Gospel writers. Third, congregants' cognitive beliefs were incongruent with their sentiments and attitudes toward the missionary mandate. It was thus concluded that even though the respondents do not have an accurate understanding of the Great Commission analogous to the teaching of the Gospels and Acts (see chapter 4), nonetheless, data from the literature review (see appendix 23) have shown that a sense of openness to missions cannot be denied. For that reason, it becomes imperative to communicate a missionary vision to the Haitian Church that reflects the intent of the Great Commission.

I have personally observed some of the contemporary enthusiasm for missions among Haitians and have heard encouraging reports from others involved in missions. One Haitian church in the Northeast United States was willing to place a missionary in Eastern Europe and Asia following a missions conference. Furthermore, I perceive that Haitian people in general have a desire to participate in missions and explore the mission fields. In many cases, when a church has organized short-term trips, people have bought their airplane tickets and participated in great numbers. On the other hand, financial issues sometimes prevent some from getting involved. The author received an e-mail from Operation Mobilization which said:

> I have received several enquiries from Haitians interested in working with Operation Mobilization. I normally reply pointing out two significant practical requirements if they are to serve with us. First, they need to have the active support and encouragement of their church leaders; without a positive reference from church leaders, we will not consider any application. Second, everyone serving with Operation Mobilization is required to raise financial support to cover at least some of their expenses. Christians from the Caribbean generally do not have to raise as much as those coming from more wealthy countries, but they still have to raise some finance. Those enquiring from Haiti have generally not replied after I have pointed out these two issues. I think that they have assumed that all their costs would be covered by our mission. (Mike Wheate, Operation Mobilization email correspondence, 28 April 2003)

It is well worth noting that the result of this research has started to make great contributions in several areas. For myself, this study not only encapsulates my learning experience at Moody Graduate School, but more importantly it has deepened my knowledge of the Great Commission and helped me strengthen my own commitment to it. On a ministry level, it has enabled me to identify the variance in understanding of the Great Commission between age groups, and between males and females, as well as to unearth five major factors that have contributed to a limited missionary vision in the Haitian Church.

Within the last two years (July 2001 – October 2003), God has enabled my church to take up the challenge of supporting four missionaries: two families in Haiti (one Haitian and one American couple), one in the USA (a Jewish couple), and one in Africa (a Korean couple). Two others are on the waiting list for 2004 (a

Spanish-American missionary for India and a French missionary to Europe). The missions' budget is also secured with 90 percent of the congregation pledging their support. Furthermore, one young woman has already committed her life to be a missionary in a cross-cultural setting. Finally, in light of this study, the congregation has voted to change the name of the Eglise Haitienne Missionnaire *(or in English, Haitian Missionary Church-HMC)* to Nouvelle Eglise Baptiste Missionnaire (NEBM) (in English, *New Missionary Baptist Church)* in order to reflect their renewed vision to reach the world.

Recommendations

The research undertaken for this study reveals that the Haitian Church (both in Haiti itself and in the diaspora (USA, Canada, France, and Latin America) has a restricted view of the Great Commission. In this section, the recommendations focus on the major points found in different parts of the research. In the theological and biblical basis (chapter I), I shared a new vision of the Great Commission articulated around three points: evangelism, disciple-making, and geographical structure. Likewise, I presented three important points discussed in the literature reviewed: how the pioneers brought the gospel to Haiti, how the gospel was received, and how the local church came to understand the Great Commission. Lastly, the findings of this survey research show that the understanding of the Church members from Evangelical and Pentecostal/Charismatic churches is contrary to the Gospel writers' intention and to Jesus' own vision. Therefore, three recommendations are given to remedy the situation.

The first recommendation has to do with the way the gospel was brought to Haitians. This recommendation concerns the theological schools, the Bible Institutes, and the mission agencies. As demonstrated in chapter 2, the emphasis was on evangelism at a National level to the exclusion of a focus on disciple-making and the geographical directives of the command. As a further complication, the gospel was presented to the Haitian people through the lens of a Western worldview, not in their "conceptual framework." Likewise, the gospel was presented in a paternalistic way rather than being incarnational or successfully contextualized. For instance, when Haitians tried to understand the Great Commission from their experience with the North American worldview, the Haitians identified missions as receiving subsidies from missionaries, carrying out compassion ministries to Haitians, and evangelizing the remote parts of Haiti. If Haitians had experienced the gospel within the framework of the Haitian culture, believers would have known that it was possible to take the gospel anywhere. Furthermore, they would have perceived providing material ingredients and sharing the gospel message as distinct from one another. *Therefore, it is suggested that the theological schools, the Bible institutes, and the mission agencies in Haiti and abroad continue to contextualize the gospel at a deeper level, to expand the students' knowledge of the missionary mandate, and to challenge them to embrace a global perspective instead of the status quo.*

One missionary e-mailed the author regarding the expediency of this thesis:

This thesis can be used as teaching materials for seminars, missions training in Bible schools and church settings to help the Haitian church grasp the biblical perspective of Christian mission -- to really understand and embrace the missionary vision of the Christian Church.

The consequences of the facts mentioned above are too important to ignore, since today's students will become spiritual leaders in the days to come. Therefore, whatever future leaders will promote or not embrace, revolves around leadership. For that reason the schools and mission agencies are in a prime position to make a huge difference in the lives of students and pastors in current service to impact the Church.

The second recommendation aims at the way the gospel was received by the Haitians. This recommendation relates to local missions and Haitian churches. The gospel was received in a context where the Haitian worldview was ignored and leaders were equipped to evangelize their own country. It is the same understanding that often proliferates in most local missions, theological schools, and the Church. As a result, the Haitian Church reaches out only to its own community in Haiti or abroad, with very little exception. Likewise, the Haitian missionaries reaching out to their own community outnumber those in full-time cross-cultural ministry. Therefore, the second recommendation proposes a forum in which local missions, Haitian National Church pastors, laypeople, theological schools, and the Church will gather to discuss this important issue. In the previous e-mail, the same missionary commented on the practicality of this thesis:

> This thesis can be used in providing helpful and practical insight to church leaders, laypeople, and missionaries, not only to discover the disease, but also to provide biblical solutions as being outlined in the Great Commission.

Insights and outcome of the forum will be published, and other avenues will be considered for making the material available to a greater audience using: a website, radio interviews in Haiti and abroad, television broadcasts, audio tapes, CD productions, and written materials. Furthermore, Moody Graduate School has already given permission to translate the research into French and Creole to reach a greater audience. Likewise, I will submit a summary article to appropriate magazines for publication. Finally, networks are being built with local missions, radio stations, and television broadcasters. Many doors are already open to make this kind of networking a reality.

The final recommendation focuses on Haitian church members' understanding of the Great Commission. The result of the research shows that most congregants of the Evangelical and Pentecostal/Charismatic churches in Chicago understand the missionary mandate as local. Likewise, they identify missions with hospital visitation, praying with prisoners in jail, or reaching out to their own countrymen for Christ. This portrait is most likely to reflect the same reality in the Haitian churches in Haiti and abroad.

The following is one way the new vision finds its application at the HMC in Evanston, Illinois. This paradigm can be modified or reproduced both in Haiti and abroad in the communication process.

The first step is to make an assessment that will determine the orientation of the church. (See *Evaluating Missions in the Local Church*, appendix 9.) The outcome of this evaluation can lead the church to a new orientation in three areas: missions exposure, mission education, and mission challenge.

GREATER MISSIONS EXPOSURE

This section covers four subdivisions: Global Missions Awareness, Missions Investigation, Missions Conferences, and Short-Term Trips.

Global Missions Awareness

In order to introduce missions in the church, I initiated Global Missions Awareness as an action step toward greater missions exposure. (See *Steps to Start a Missions Ministry in Your Church*, appendix 10.)

The first step in preparing for Global Missions Awareness was to choose 10 countries from around the world as the object of our prayers. As pastor, I worked with those taking our missions education course to make these selections. The nations selected were shown on a world map to help the congregation visualize their exact locations.

Starting May 4, 2003, members of the congregation began researching these nations according to a schedule we built. Four weeks ahead of time, a person is chosen to research one country of his or her choice and present the findings to help the congregation pray more effectively. Their presentation is made in the language of the participant's choice (English, French, or Creole). So far, the people are very excited and looking forward to the presentations.

This schedule is going very well. The book *Operation World* (Johnstone and Mandryk 2001) (in French and English), along with specific websites, will be made available to the people doing the research. The following is an example of the schedule for each Sunday of the month:

First Sunday	Kids from 5 – 11 years old
Second Sunday	Youth 12 – 18 years old
Third Sunday	Younger adults 19 – 30 years old
Fourth Sunday	Adults 31 – 59 years old
Fifth Sunday	Seniors 60 years old and over

At the beginning of 2003, the HMC began allocating 5 to 10 minutes each Sunday to pray for different countries and leaders around the world. Scriptures such as 1 Timothy 2:1-4 or Matthew 9:35-38 were projected and read to support their prayer. Moreover, prayer is embedded at both the individual and corporate level for missions endeavors. Likewise, one section in the weekly bulletin is reserved for missions. Included are: a list of missionaries the church is in contact with, important mission information posted on missions such as websites (example www.gmi.org/mislinks), statistics about different needs around the world, quotes, and so forth. Furthermore, the third Sunday of each month is set aside as Missions Sunday. On that day, qualified guest speakers (missionaries, pastors, etc.) are invited to preach and share their testimonies. Likewise, mission reports are given from different mission fields around the world, and the congregation is kept informed through correspondence with missionaries in the field.

Some members have put together a drama team and write their own scripts. Regarding their work, one missionary who was part of the congregation e-mailed the author:

I definitely believe that you have made a HUGE difference in making your congregation aware of the need for missions and I commend you!...You of course had a passion to see missions presented through regular missions conferences and prayer for missions each Sunday. Also by mentioning the missionaries in the bulletin each Sunday, kept it in the people's thoughts.

Those small steps symbolize concrete actions taken for a greater exposure, to promote missions and keep it alive in the church (see, *Issues in Communicating Missions to the Local Church*, appendix 11). The result can create a great impact on a congregation that is enthused for missions and prays to God to touch the hearts of other ethnic groups around the world.

MISSIONS INVESTIGATION

As part of their investigation into missions, our church leadership plans to visit various mission headquarters to learn about what each organization is doing regarding missions. Likewise, these leaders can attend missions conferences at affiliate churches or other institutions such as: Moody Bible Institute (www.moody.edu), Advancing Churches in Missions Commitment (ACMC)[12], or Antioch Network annual conference (www.antiochnetwork.org).

Furthermore, the leadership of the church can subscribe to missions journals or periodicals such as: Mission Frontiers[13]; Evangelism and Missions Information Service (EMIS)[14]; and Evangelism Missions Quarterly (EMQ)[15].

Finally, members are encouraged and challenged to take classes at a Bible institute or seminary. God has blessed the effort of the HMC through encouragement and challenge of the members to take classes at a Bible institute or at the seminary level. As a result, three people are taking evening classes at Moody Bible Institute and Wheaton College for further training. Others are planning to do the same.

---

[12] www.acmc.org; www.Davidmays.org
[13] www.missionfrontiers.org
[14] www.gospelcom.net/bgc/emis/
[15] www.gospelcom.net/bgc/emis/emqpg.htm

Missions Conference

Since the inception of the HMC, an annual missions conference has been included among the activities. (See *Steps to a Good Missions Conference*, appendix 12.) We have invited different missionaries and agencies to participate. Flags of many nations are on display with books on missions available for participants to acquire. Likewise, we organized a related workshop, and at the end of the each conference, an altar call is made. Last year, five young people from the HMC committed to missionary service as a result of the missions conferences, and one is preparing for cross-cultural missions following college.

More than one missionary interviewed (see appendix 7) said "my first encounter with missions was during a missions conference." One missionary who attended the HMC wrote this e-mail to the author:…"Your dedication to have missions conferences and present missionaries frequently in the service has, I'm sure, caused them to think."

Recently, one Haitian missionary shared the excitement of some congregants at a missions conference:

Eglise Baptiste du Tabernacle [*in Haiti*] is about to celebrate their 30th anniversary in April 2003. Last month they organized their first Missions Conference, and I was invited to be the first speaker on the opening night. Over 100 persons have returned pledge cards, and one older saint said he wished he was 17 again so he could go as a missionary somewhere. UFM, Youth with a Mission, and Campus Crusade were some of the missions/evangelistic agencies represented at this conference.

This illustration is a precise case in point that can foster the vision and set a new direction for a congregation. Therefore, it is never too late to start.

Short-Term Trips

Short-term trips represent one of the best means available both for exposing pastors and church members to the needs in the mission field. In 1999, the HMC organized its first short-term trip to Haiti with its two pastors and five church members. (See, *Issues for a Short-Term Missions Policy*, appendix 13.) The experience was overwhelming for the team who participated, but equally for the members of the congregation when they received the reports of what God had done through seven people. As a result of the trip, 262 souls came to the Lord in 10 days.

Later, the author learned that the presence of both pastors (HMC) in that group was impressive for the local missions visited in Haiti. More importantly, that trip set the stage for more missionary endeavors; in two years' time, one of the pastors went as a full-time missionary in the field. As a direct application of what was learned in the global vision of the Great Commission, the HMC is currently praying while it considers three invitations to participate in cross-cultural missions trips.

Missions Education

The third step refers to missions education. One key to succeed with such endeavors has to do with leadership involvement. In order for missions to take root in the life of the local church, the pastor must see its importance. He is a key player in the communication process once he understands his role. (See *The Pastor's Roles in Missions*, appendix 14.)

To get started, it is suggested that during the first year, the pastor would take the initiative to invite guest speakers while he also preaches on missions and stewardship. (See *Principals for Influencing Individuals for Missions*, appendix 15; and *Biblical Stewardship,* appendix 16.) The pastor will need the support of the congregation in that direction. (See *How to Help Your Pastor in Missions,* appendix 17.)

In February, 2003, the HMC started a course on missions once a month with 15 volunteers (youth and adults) who wanted to learn more about missions and stewardship. (See an illustration, *Sermon Outline*, on the Great Commission appendix 18.) The author designed this course to teach the basis of missions as seen in the Gospels and Acts and to educate on stewardship as well. The materials presented in chapter 1 of this book, "Theological and Biblical Basis of This Study," were used for that purpose. In that informal setting, congregants were eager to learn about missions, ask questions, and give testimony that further clarified their perspectives of missions.

In the second year, the pastor would lead studies on missions as related in the Epistles and Revelation, as well as the biographies of some missionaries. Likewise, the person in charge will select key leaders (youth and adults) to attend Sonlife seminars[16].

In the third year, the church will study missions in the Old Testament and work at building a missions committee. (See, *Keys for Missions Committee Operation*, appendix 19.)

In the fourth year, another survey will be conducted to assess the church's understanding of the Great Commission following the above steps.

Mission Challenges

The fourth step needed to raise awareness of global missions has to do with Missions Challenge, which is a big part of the communication process. What God has done with the Mission Challenge in Chicago (HMC) and other places can happen to other churches as well. As the author is taking leadership to teach, preach, and participate in support of missionaries of the church, God touches the heart of the congregation to meet the needs in the field. Likewise, some have been given the opportunity to visit missionaries in the field as a way to encourage and minister to them.

---

[16] www.sonlife.com

On the third Sunday of January 2003, the author challenged the congregation through an altar call to take a more active part in missions. As a result, ten members responded positively. They are the ones who have become the nucleus for the missions' class once a month. God has used the preaching against materialism to cause 70 percent of the congregation to support more than one missionary.

The final step is to challenge and recruit others to be part of a missions committee. (See *The Job of the Missions Committee*, appendix 20.) After workers are enlisted, a retreat would be organized to nail down some specific objectives. (See, *Steps for a Missions Planning Retreat*, appendix 21; and *Missions Management Basics*, appendix 22.)

Through groaning prayers and seeking His face, the author has received confirmation from the Lord about a ministry (VIGCOM) which is the outflow of the thesis that inspired this book. That ministry will serve to help carry out that task of building a new awareness of the Great Commission, particularly within the Haitian Church. A summary of "VIGCOM" is outlined in appendix 27 and can also be checked out on the web at (www.vigcom.org).

Finally, there are salient issues that my thesis and this book did not deal with that might be the subject of further research and needs assessments:

(1) A survey among the Haitian pastors could be conducted to find out their perspectives about the reason for the lack of Haitian missionaries around the world and discover their major concerns.

(2) Studies can be performed to determine why Haitians are more interested in going to Africa as missionaries. Does it have to do with language or ethnic affinity?

(3)   Other important questions could be raised, such as the following:

    a.   What impact does language or finances play in the decision-making process as a Haitian looks into becoming a missionary?

    b.   What are the family issues that could hinder Haitian missions' involvement, such as: marriage, debt, education, children, career, and parents?

    c.   What would be the best curriculum for teaching missions in the local churches?

(4)   It would be of great importance to have a credible organization or institution facilitating short-term trips for pastors or key leaders for missions' exposure. Criteria of selection would be needed for such choices.

(5)   Studies can be performed to gain useful statistical data on Haitian pastors, congregation memberships, affiliates, and the percentage of believers in the Haitian diaspora.

Finally, when everything is said and done, may the result of this research be used by God to bring honor and glory to Him and Him alone - Soli Deo Gloria!

BIBLIOGRAPHY

Amertil, Nino. Short-Term Missionary to Africa. 2 October 2003. Interview by author. Notes. Chicago, Illinois.

Anderson, Gerald H. *The Theology Of The Christian Mission.* New York, NY: McGraw-Hill Book Company, 1961.

Araujo, Alex. *"Retooling the Future," Evangelical Missions Quarterly*, Volume 29, no. 4, October 1993, (362-363).

Badgero, Ray. "Biculturalism." Class Notes of Moody Bible Institute. Spring 1997.

Banks, William L. *In Search of the Great Commission.* Chicago, Illinois: Moody Press, 1991.

Baptist Haiti Mission. Accessed March 4, 2003. Available from: http://www.bhm.org/ministry/stats.htm; internet.

Barker, Kenneth L. *The NIV Study Bible.* Grand Rapids, Michigan: Zondervan, 1995.

Barna, George. Accessed March 4, 2003. Available from: http://www.barna.org/cgi-bin/PageCategory.asp?CategoryID=18.internet.

_____. *The Power of Vision.* Ventura, California: Regal Books, 1992.

_____. *Turning Vision into Action.* Ventura, California: Regal Books, 1996.

Barrett, David. B.; George T. Kurian, and Todd M. Johnson. *World Christian Encyclopedia: A Comparative Survey of*

Churches and Religions in the Modern World, Volume 1.
New York, New York: Oxford University Press, 2001.

Berthole, Margery. Short-Term Missionary to Africa. 10
September 2003. Interview by author. Notes. Chicago,
Illinois.

Biblical Stewardship. Accessed April 7, 2003. Available from:
http://www.generousgiving.org/page.asp?sec; internet.

Bloomberg, Craig L. *An Introduction and Survey: Jesus and the
Gospels.* Nashville, TN: Broadman and Holman Publishers,
1997.

_____. *Neither Poverty nor Riches.* Downers Grove, IL:
Intervarsity Press, 2000.

Bodley, John H. "An Anthropological Perspective," from *Cultural
Anthropology: Tribes, States, and the Global System.*
McGraw-Hill Humanities/Social Sciences/Languages; 1994.
Accessed 21 July 21 2003 from: http://www.wsu.edu:8001/
vcwsu/commons/topics/culture/ culture-definitions/bodley-
text.html; internet.

Brea, Jorge A. "Population Dynamics in Latin America."
Population Bulletin, Vol. 58, no. 1, (March 2003), 7.

British Broadcasting Corporation. Accessed April 30, 2003.
Available from: http://news.bbc.co.uk.go/pr/fr/-/2/hi/americas
/29857.stm.

Burgess, Stanley M. *The New International Dictionary of
Pentecostal and Charismatic Movements.* Grand Rapids,
Michigan: Zondervan, 2002.

Burgess, Stanley M. and Gary B. McGee. *Dictionary of Pentecostal and Charismatic Movements.* Grand Rapids, Michigan: Zondervan, 1989.

Cadet, Pierre R., Pastor and Haitian Missionary from Nouvelle Eglise Baptiste Missionnaire with EBM. 19 December 2002. Interview by author. Notes. Chicago, Illinois.

Carver, William Owen. *Missions in the Plan of the Ages.* New York, NY: Fleming H. Revell Company, 1909.

Casséus, Jules. *Perspectives Missionnaires.* Port-au-Prince, Haiti: La Presse Evangelique, 1997.

_____. President of Université Chrétienne Du Nord D'Haiti *(Christian University of North Haiti).* 14 October 2002. Interview by author. Notes. Chicago, Illinois.

Church of the Nazarene in Haiti. Accessed March 24, 2003. Available from: http://www.caribbeannazarene.org; internet.

Cole, R. Alan. *Tyndale New Testament Commentaries – Mark.* Grand Rapids, Michigan: Eerdmans Publishing Company, 1993.

Coleman, Robert E. *The Great Commission Lifestyle.* Old Tappan, New Jersey: Fleming H. Revell Company, 1992.

_____. *The Master Plan of Discipleship.* Old Tappan, New Jersey: Fleming H. Revell Company, 1987.

Desamour, Thelemaque. Former Missionary to Africa. 26 September2003. Interview by author. Notes. Chicago, Illinois.

Deshommes, Pierre. Former Missionary to Africa. 17 September 2003. Interview by author. NotesChicago, Illinois.

Destiné, Jonias. Recteur Université Lumière and Haitian Missionary with MEBSH. 13 May 2003. E-mail correspondence with author.

Destournel, Suzie. Short-Term Haitian Missionary from Eglise Evangelique Baptiste Bethesda with AIM. 13 August 2003. Interview by author. Notes. Chicago, Illinois.

Eléazard, Marie Myrtha. Short-Term Haitian Missionary from Eglise Evangelique Baptiste Bethesda with AIM. 20 January 2003. Interview by author. Notes. Chicago, Illinois.

Escobar, Samuel. "Evangelical in Latin America." *Evangelical Missions Quarterly*, Volume 39, no. 3, July 2003, (288-289).

Fils-Aimé, Jean. *L'inculturation du Protestantisme Au contexte du Vodou haitien: Plaidoyer pour l'haitianisation des églises évangéliques d'Haiti.* Ph. D. dissertation, Université de Montréal. 2002.

Firmin, Jean Wiclef. Short-Term Haitian Missionary from Eglise Biblique Pierre Angulaire with AIM. 24 January 2003. Interview by author. Notes. Chicago, Illinois.

Fombrun, Odette Roy. *Histoire D'Haiti: Des Origines à l'Independance.* Port-Au-Prince: Imprimerie Henri Deschamps, 1986.

_____. *Histoire d'Haiti: De l'Independance à nos jours.* Port-Au-Prince: Imprimerie Henri Deschamps, 1986.

Fontus, Fritz. *Effective Communication of the Gospel in Haiti.* Pembroke Pines, Florida: Fritz Fontus, 2001.

_____. Pastor and former Missionary with ABS/UBS. 31 October and 2002 and 2 May 2003. E-mail correspondence and conversation with author. Chicago, Illinois.

France, R.T. *Tyndayle New Testament Commentaries - Matthew.* Grand Rapids, Michigan: Eerdmans Publishing Company, 1985.

Frizen, Edwin L. Jr. *Seventy-Five Years of IFMA.* Pasadena, California: William Carey Library, 1992.

Gabelein, Frank E. *The Expositor's Bible Commentary,* Vol. 8, (Matthieu, Mark, Luke). Grand Rapids, Michigan: Zondervan Corporation, 1984.

Georgeon, Jamil. Pastor, Eglise Baptiste du Rédempteur d'expression Française, New York, NY. 14 October 2002. Interview by author Notes. Chicago, Illinois.

Glover, Robert Hall. *The Bible Basis Of Missions.* Chicago, Illinois: Moody Press, 1964.

Gonzáles, Justo L. *The Story of Christianity.* Vol. 2, (The Reformation to the Present Day). Peabody, MA: Prince Press, 2001.

Guthrie, Donald. *New Testament Introduction.* Downers Grove, IL: Intervarsity Press, 1990.

Haitian Institute of Statistics and Information. Accessed May 19, 2003. Available from: http://www.haitimedical.com/ haiti_stats.htm; internet.

Heneise, Ivah T. *Pioneers of Light.* Kearney, NE: Morris Publishing, 1999.

Hesselgrave, David J. *Communicating Christ Cross-Culturally.* Grand Rapids, Michigan: Zondervan, 1991.

Hiebert, Paul G. *Anthropological Insights for Missionaries.* Grand Rapids, MI: Baker Books, 2001.

Hodges, Melvin L. *The Indigenous Church*. Springfield, Missouri: Gospel Publishing House, 1976.

Jean Baptiste, Matthieu. Evangelist. Haitian Evangelical Crusade Association. 14 October 2002. Interview by author. Notes. Chicago, Illinois.

Jean Pierre, Mullery. Pastor, Beraca Baptist Church in Brooklyn, New York. 2 October 2003. Email correspondence.

Jeanty, Edner A. *"Le Christianisme en Haiti"*. Port-au-Prince: La Presse Evangelique, 1990.

_____. Pastor and Former Professor of STEP. 27 April 2000. Interview by author. Notes. Chicago, Illinois.

_____. Former Missionary with Unevangelized Field Mission (UFM). 27 July 2002 – 7 April 2003. Conversation and e-mail correspondence with author.

Jenkins, Philip. *The Next Christendom: The Coming of Global Christianity*. New York, New York: Oxford University Press, 2002.

Jeune, Chavannes. President MEBSH, Haiti. 2002. Interview by author, Chicago, Illinois. 5 November. Tape recording.

Jeune, Vladimir. *"Upper Class and Evangelism."* Chicago, Illinois, 7 March 2003. Email communication.

Joachin, Rolland. Former Missionary to Africa. 17 September 2003. Interview by author. Notes. Chicago, Illinois.

Johnson, Hammon A. *The Growing Church in Haiti*. Coral Gables, Florida: West Indies Mission. 1970.

Johnstone, Patrick. *Operation World, English Full-Text Database Software,* [CD-ROM] (Waynesboro, GA: Paternoster-Publishing, 2001).

Johnstone, Patrick and Mandryk Jason. *Operation World.* Waynesboro, GA: Paternoster, 2001.

Kane, J. Hebert. *Understanding Christian Missions.* Grand Rapids, Michigan: Baker Book House, 1991.

_____. *Christian Missions In Biblical Perspective.* Grand Rapids, Michigan: Baker Book House, 1976.

_____. *Global View of Christian Missions.* Grand Rapids, Michigan: Baker Book House, 1972.

Keener, Craig S. *The IVP New Testament Commentary Series: Matthew.* Downers Grove, IL: Intervarsity Press, 1997.

Lacombe, Frantz. *God's Intervention in the Tower of Babel Story Surmises a Problem* (an unpublished thesis, Old Testament Biblical Theology, Moody Graduate School, Chicago, Illinois, 1999).

_____. *A Biblical Theology of the Book of James*, (an unpublished thesis, New Testament Biblical Theology, Moody Graduate School, Chicago, Illinois, 2000).

_____. *Do the Haitian Evangelical Churches in Chicago Have a Missionary Vision?* (an unpublished thesis, Seminar of Church History, Moody Graduate School, Chicago, Illinois, 2000).

_____. *A Biblical Theology of the Gospel of* Mark, (an unpublished thesis, Biblical Theology of the Gospels, Moody Graduate School, Chicago, Illinois, 2000).

_____. *Growing a Healthy Church*, (an unpublished thesis, Sonlife Ministries, Chicago, Illinois, 2000).

Lacombe, Hebert. *Détresse Psychologique et Suicidalité: Associations avec la Religiosité et la Spiritualité des Québécois* (an unpublished dissertation, Ph. D. Candidate, Université du Québec à Trois-Rivières, Québec, Canada, 2003).

Latourette, Kenneth Scott. *A History of Christianity. Volumse I & II.* Peabody, MA: Prince Press, 2000.

Lazer, Jeannette. Missionary with Interact Missions. 29 January 2002. Interview by author Notes. Chicago, Illinois.

Leyburn, James. *The Haitian People.* New Haven, CN: Yale University Press, 1966.

Lilite, Jean O., 14 October 2002. Pastor of Eglise Haitienne de la Grace (CMA). Interview by author. Notes. Chicago, Illinois.

Lindsell, Harold. *The Church's Worldwide Mission.* Waco, Texas: Word Books, 1966.

Lingenfelter, Shwerwood G. and Marvin K. Mayers. *Ministering Cross-Culturally: An Incarnational Model for Personal Relationships.* Grand Rapids, MI: Baker Book House Company, 1996.

Louis, Fredrine. Short-Term Haitian Missionary from Eglise Evangelique Baptiste Bethesda,. 14 August 2003. Interview by author. Notes. Chicago, Illinois.

Martin, Alfred. *Biblical Stewardship.* Loizeaux Brothers. 1991.

Mays, David. *Stuff You Need to Know about Doing Missions in Your Church.* Accessed May 19, 2003. Available from: http://www.davidmays.org/Current-BN/MoreStuff.pdf

Moreau, A. Scott. *Evangelical Dictionary of World Missions.* Grand Rapids, Michigan: Baker Book House, 2000.

Morissette, Georges. Pastor of Eglise de Dieu d'Outremont. 25 September 2003. Interview by author. Notes. Chicago, Illinois.

Morris, Leon. *The New International Commentary on The New Testament: The Gospel According to John*: Grand Rapids, MI: Eerdmans Publishing, 1992.

Noel, Claude. Former President of CEEH. 30 July 2003. Interview by author. Notes. Chicago, Illinois.

Olson, C. Gordon. *What in the World is God Doing?* Cedar Knolls, NJ: Global Gospel Publishers, 1993.

Peters, George W. *A Biblical Theology of Missions.* Chicago, Illinois: Moody Press, 1972.

Piper, John. *Let the Nations Be Glad!* Grand Rapids, MI: Baker Books, 1993.

Population Reference Bureau. Accessed May 19, 2003. Available from: http://www.prb.org/pdf/WorldPopulationDS02_Eng.pdf; internet.

Romain, Charles-Poisset. *Le Protestantisme Dans La Société Haitienne : Contribution à l'étude d'une religion (Protestantism in the Haitian Society: Contribution to the Study of a Religion).* Port-Au-Prince: Imprimerie Henri Deschamps, 1986.

Saint-Germain, Brezil. Former President of MEBSH. 13 August 2003. Interview by author. Notes. Chicago, Illinois.

Saint-Louis, Félix. Former Missionary with MEBSH.
20 September 2003. Interview by author. Notes. Chicago,
Illinois.

See, Roger and Karen. Missionaries with Unevangelized Field
Mission (UFM). 13 April 2000. Conversation with author.
Notes. Chicago, Illinois.

Seventh-Day Adventist. Accessed March 7, 2003. Available from:
http://volunteers.gc.adventist.org/avs/ avsdatabase /Pages
/Countries /Profiles /SDA%20Presence/preshaiti.htm; internet.

Siewert, John A. and Welliver, Dotsey. *Mission Handbook (U.S.
and Canadian Christian Ministries Overseas).* Wheaton, IL:
Billy Graham Center, 2001.

Smith, Donald K. A Path Through the Confusion of Culture.
Class Notes.

Sogaard, Viggo. *Research in Church and Mission.* Pasadena,
California: William Carey Library, 1996.

Spader, Dann. *Growing A Healthy Church: The Strategy of Jesus.*
Elburn, Illinois: Sonlife, 1998.

_____. *Growing A Healthy Church, Three: Advanced Training.*
Elburn, Illinois: Sonlife, 1997.

Spader, Dann, and Gary Mayes. *The Everyday Commission.*
Wheaton, Illinois: Harold Shaw Publishers, 1994.

_____. *Growing A Healthy Church.* Chicago, Illinois: Moody
Press, 1991.

Speer, Robert E. *Christianity and the Nations.* Chicago, Illinois:
Fleming H. Revell Company, 1910.

Storch, Charles. Article in *Chicago Tribune*, 21 October 1999, section 5, pages 1 and 13.

Stott, John R. W. *Christian Mission in the Modern World.* Downers Grove, Illinois: Intervarsity Press, 1975.

Sutherland, James W. *African American Underrepresentation in Intercultural Missions: Perceptions of Black Missionaries and the Theory of Survival Security.* Ph. D. dissertation, Trinity Evangelical Divinity School. 1998.

Thomas, Jean Baptiste. Pastor, Eglise Baptiste d'Expression Française de Brooklyn, New York, NY. 14 October 2002. Interview by author Notes. Chicago, Illinois.

United Nation Statistics. Accessed April 9, 2003. Available from http://www.eclac.org/publicaciones/Estadisticas/8/LCG2118PB/c-2-I.pdf; internet.

U.S. Center For World Mission. *Vision for the Nations.* Pasadena, CA: U.S Center for World Mission, 2001.

Van Rheenen, Gailyn. *Communicating Christ in Animistic Contexts.* Grand Rapids, Michigan: Baker Book House, 1991.

Vedrine, Soliny. Pastor, Eglise Baptiste Missionnaire De Boston and Coordinateur International Vision Globale du Protestantisme dans le Milieu Haitien. 28 June 2002. interview by author. Tape recording. Upsilinty, Michigan. .

Vericain, Pierre. Short-Term Missionary from La Bible Parle. 3 April 2003. Interview by author. Notes. Chicago, Illinois.

Verkuyl, Johannes. *Contemporary Missiology.* Grand Rapids, Michigan: Eerdmans Publishing Company, 1978.

Vicedom, George F. *The Mission of God.* St. Louis, Missouri:
Concordia Publishing House, 1965.

Walker, Rosemary E. *The Communication of A Cross-Cultural
Missionary Vision To National Churches.* M.A. Thesis,
Columbia Biblical Seminary and Graduate School of Missions.
1993.

_____. Regional Coordinator. Africa Inland Mission, Canada.
21 January 2003. Interview by author. Notes. Chicago,
Illinois.

Walker, Edwin. *The Importance of Worldview Discipleship in
Planting Healthy Reproducing Churches,"* (an unpublished
work, paper presented at a special meeting with Haitian leaders
of MEBSH, Haiti, December 2002).

_____. "Mission Structures and Management Principles for the
21st Century" (an unpublished work, paper presented at a
special meeting with Haitian leaders of MEBSH, Haiti,
December 2002).

_____. "Global Sharing of Resources: Special Task Force Study
Edition" (an unpublished work, paper presented at a special
meeting with Haitian leaders of MEBSH, Haiti, December
2002).

_____. "Mission Structures and Management Principles for the 21st
Century" (an unpublished work, paper presented at a special
meeting with Haitian leaders of MEBSH, Haiti, December,
2002).

_____. Former Missionary in Haiti with World Team. 2003.
Correspondence and conversation with author, Chicago,
Illinois. 26 March. Notes.

Weber, Steve. *The Relationship of the Various Types of Relief and Development Philosophies to the Growth of the Church in Haiti* (Th. M). *Fuller Theological Seminary, 1980.*

Weick, D. Elie. Pastor of Seventh Day Bethlehem Adventist Church. 11 September 2003. Interview by author. Notes. Chicago, Illinois.

Wheate, Mike. *Operation Mobilization.* 28 April 2003. Email correspondence.

Wilkins, Michael J. *Following the Master.* Grand Rapids, Michigan: Zondervan Publishing House, 2000.

Winter, Ralph D., and Steven C. Hawthorne. *Perspectives on the World Christian Movement.* Pasadena, California: William Carey Library, 1999.

World Bank. Accessed April 9, 2003. Available from: http://devdata.worldbank.org/external/ CPProfile.asp?CCODE=HTI&PTYPE=CP; internet.

World Evangelical Alliance. Accessed September 27, 2003. Available from http://www.worldevangelical.org/ persec_haiti_26aug03 .html ; internet.

World Factbook. Accessed October 4, 2003. Available from http://www.infoplease.com/ipa/A0748754.html

Zuck, Roy B. *A Biblical Theology of the New Testament.* Chicago, Illinois: Moody Press, 1994.

RIPE NOW!

APPENDIX 1:
Diverse Definitions of Culture

Topical:	Culture consists of everything on a list of topics, or categories, such as social organization, religion, or economy
Historical:	Culture is social heritage, or tradition, that is passed on to future generations
Behavioral:	Culture is shared, learned human behavior, a way of life
Normative:	Culture is ideals, values, or rules for living
Functional:	Culture is the way humans solve problems of adapting to the environment or living together
Mental:	Culture is a complex of ideas, or learned habits, that inhibit impulses and distinguish people from animals
Structural:	Culture consists of patterned and interrelated ideas, symbols, or behaviors
Symbolic:	Culture is based on arbitrarily assigned meanings that are shared by a society

SOURCE:

Bodley, John H. Bodley, "An Anthropological Perspective," from *Cultural Anthropology: Tribes, States, and the Global System.* McGraw-Hill Humanities/Social Sciences/Languages; 1994. Information accessed through http://www.wsu.edu:8001/vcwsu/commons/topics/culture/culture-definitions/bodley-text.html.

APPENDIX 2:
American Protestant Mission Agencies in Haiti

#	Agency Name	Year Begun
1	Seventh-Day Adventists	1905
2	American Baptist Churches USA	1923
3	Society of St. Margaret	1927
4	Church of God of Prophecy	1931
5	Church of God World Missions	1933
6	Baptist Mid-Missions	1934
7	World Team	1936
8	UFM International	1943
9	Evangelical Bible Mission	1943
10	Baptist Haiti Mission	1943
11	Assemblies of God	1945
12	Child Evangelism Fellowship	1946
13	Wesleyan World Missions	1948
14	Church of the Nazarene	1950
16	Pentecostal Church of God	1952
17	Rehoboth Ministries, Inc	1952
18	OMS International, Inc	1958
19	World Gospel Mission	1962
20	World-Wide Missions	1962
21	Christian Service International	1963
22	Free Methodist World Missions	1964
23	United Pentecostal Church International	1966
24	Have Christ Will Travel Ministries	1966
25	International Child Care	1966
26	Churches of God General Conference	1967
27	Macedonia World Baptist Missions	1967
28	Compassion International Inc.	1968
29	Allegheny Wesleyan Methodist Missions	1969

#	Agency Name	Year Begun
30	Good Shepherd Ministries	1973
31	Ministries In Action	1974
32	Presbyterian Church (USA)	1974
33	Christian Reformed Relief	1975
34	National Baptist Convention of America	1975
35	International Pentecostal Holiness Church	1976
36	New Life League International	1976
37	Campus Crusade for Christ	1977
38	World Concern	1977
39	Larry Jones International Ministries	1979
40	Mission Possible	1979
41	Foursquare Missions International	1981
42	Habitat for Humanity International	1981
43	Harvest	1981
44	Medical Ambassadors International	1981
45	Mission Aviation Fellowship	1981
46	Baptist Bible Fellowship International	1982
47	Hope for the Hungry	1982
48	International Partnership Ministries	1982
49	Mission to the Americas	1982
50	Christian Reformed World	1985
51	STEM Ministries	1985
52	Baptist World Mission	1986
53	Elim Fellowship World Missions	1986
54	FOCAS	1986
55	Global Strategy Mission Association	1988
56	Reciprocal Ministries International	1988
57	Global Outreach, Ltd.	1989
58	Globe Missionary Evangelism	1990
59	Christian Aid Ministries	1991
60	Missionary Ventures International	1992
61	Resurrection Churches & Ministries	1992
62	Christian Church (Disciples of Christ)	1992

#	Agency Name	Year Begun
	Division of Ove	
63	Barnabas Ministries, Inc.	1993
64	ECHO	1993
65	Evangelical Baptist Missions	1993
66	Heart of God Ministries	1994
67	Floresta USA, Inc	1995
68	Open Door Baptist Missions	1995
69	Childcare International	----
70	Christian Aid Mission	----
71	East West Ministries	----
72	FARMS International, Inc.	----
73	Hope Bible Mission, Inc.	----
74	Missions Outreach International	----
75	United Church Board World Ministries	----
76	Evangelical Congregational Church Division of Missions	1997
77	Youth With A Mission	1998
78	Church of the Brethren	1998
79	Evangelical Free Church Mission	1998
80	Friends for Missions	1998
81	Haiti Gospel Mission	1998
82	Baptist International Missions	1998
83	Christian Service International (CSI) Ministries	1998
84	International Fellowship of Evangelical Students	1998
85	ISOH/Impact	1998
86	Southern Baptist Convention - IMB	1998
87	Mission Society for United Methodists	1998
88	New Missions in Haiti	1998
89	Mennonite Central Committee	1998
90	Churches of Christ (USA)	1999
91	Christian Blind Mission International	2000

#	Agency Name	Year Begun
92	Christian Crusade/Crusade of Christ	2000

APPENDIX 3:
Canadian Protestant Mission Agencies in Haiti

#	Agency Name	Year Begun
1	World Team Canada	1936
2	UFM International in Canada	1943
3	OMS International - Canada	1964
4	Mennonite Economic	1972
5	Emmanuel International	1978
6	Christian Reformed Relief	1986
7	International Child Care	1986
8	Pentecostal Assemblies	1996
9	Global Outreach Mission	----

SOURCE:

Patrick Johnstone, *Operation World, English Full-Text Database Software,* [CD-ROM] (Waynesboro, GA: Paternoster-Publishing, 2001).

APPENDIX 4:
Other Protestant Mission Agencies in Haiti

#	Agency Name	Country	Year Begun
1	Zending En Gemeente	Netherlands	1990
2	Département Evangélique Français D'action Apostolique	France	1992
3	Servicio Cristiano Internacional	Dominican Republic	1995
4	Comunidad Misionera Hosanna	Panama	1996
5	Salvation Army	Norway	1998
6	Vereinigte Deutsche Missionshilfe	Germany	1999
7	Verband Deutscher Mennonitengemeinden	Germany	2000
8	Christian Blind Mission International	Germany	2000
9	Heart For Haiti	Netherlands	2000
10	Deutsche Missionsgemeinschaft	Germany	2000
11	Christliche Fachkräfte International	Germany	2000

SOURCE:

Patrick Johnstone, *Operation World, English Full-Text Database Software,* [CD-ROM] (Waynesboro, GA: Paternoster-Publishing, 2001).

APPENDIX 5: National Mission Agencies (1817- 2000)

#	Name of Agency	Founded	Congr. #		Membership		Affiliate	
			1968	**2000**	**1968**	**2000**	**1968**	**2000**
1	Eglise Méthodiste d'Haiti	1817	123*	380	2,757*	9,500	11,028*	23,000
2	Eglise Méthodiste Episcopale Africaine	1823	89*	12	8,000*	1,100	15,000*	4,400
3	Eglise Episcopale d'Haiti	1861	176*	367	15,092*	31,532	38,452*	105,000
4	Eglise Baptiste Stricte Jacmel	1885 ?	30	---	17,000	---	28,000	---
5	Mission Adventiste D'Haiti	1905	79*	280	34,657*	180,000	60,000*	360,000
6	Loth Carey Baptist Mission	1921	16	---	2,131	---	4,944	---
7	Convention Baptiste D'Haiti	1924	669*	453	36,000*	84,599	80,000*	300,000
8	Eglise de Dieu en Christ	1929	96*	140	10,697*	21,000	15,000*	44,000
9	Eglise de Dieu (Cleveland)	1934	220*	307	18,839*	61,236	56,515*	140,000
10	Mission Evangelique Baptiste d'Haiti (UEBH)	1936	217*	420	10,113*	19,000	35,000*	38,000
11	Eglise Baptiste Eben-Ezer	1936	50*	125	4,000*	10,000	8,000*	20,000
12	Mission Evangelique Baptiste du Sud Haiti	1936	181	407	19,910	39,862	30,485	100,577
13	Eglise de Dieu de la Prophétie	1938	249*	310	23,932*	22,000	59,830*	45,000
14	Petit Troupeau	1940	2	---	280	---	1,230	---
15	Eglise de la Foi Apostolique M.	1941	22	---	10,000	---	20,000	---
16	Mission Baptiste Haitienne	1942	4*	8	530*	900	1,000*	1,600
17	Mission Eben-Ezer	1942	83	---	12,000	---	40,000	---
18	Eglise (Mission) Baptiste	1943	115	325*	5,572	17,646**	24,000	70,000**

#	Name of Agency	Founded	Congr. #		Membership		Affiliate	
			1968	2000	1968	2000	1968	2000
	Conservatrice			*				
19	Eglise Wesleyenne d'Haiti	1943	148*	80	2,531*	4,000	8,079*	10,500
20	Eglise Baptiste de P-A-P (II)	1944	8	---	2,400	---	4,000	---
21	Baptist Mid-Mission	1946	10	---	570	---	700	---
22	Mission Evangelique par la Foi d'Haiti	1948	12	---	345	---	840	---
23	Eglise de Dieu Mission Pentecostale Libre	1949	5	---	1,000	---	1,555	---
24	Eglise Evangélique d'Haiti	1950	76*	20	688*	3,000	2,915*	12,000
25	Armée du Salut	1950	15*	36	500*	1,200	1,000*	2,400
26	Eglise du Nazaréen	1950	260*	480	19,826*	78,000	30,000*	260,000
27	Armée du Christ	1951	5	---	125	---	850	---
28	Eglise de Dieu de la Pentecôte	1953	196	140	2,940	15,000	5,880	30,000
29	Croisade Evangélique Mondiale	1956	22*	89	2,000*	8,000	4,000*	16,000
30	Société d'Unité Spirit. Evg.	1957	1	---	500	---	3,000	---
31	Les Assemblée du Saint Esprit	1957	21	---	1,075	---	2,280	---
32	Les Assemblée de Dieu	1958	34	220	1,683	30,000	4,600	42,000
33	Mission Evangelique Assemblée des Elus	1958	7	---	930	---	1,891	---
34	Eglise de Dieu d'Haiti	1962	5	---	33	---	700	---
35	Eglise Pentecostale Unie	1962	125*	429	4,300*	30,000	10,000*	40,000
36	Eglise Méthodiste Libre	1964	21*	58	1,165*	15,000	2,000*	32,000
37	Eglise Mennonite	1966	4	10	74	520	190	1,400
38	Eglise Missionnaire	---	16*	280	1,840*	7,000	3,496*	12,000
39	Eglise de Dieu (Anderson)	---	125	429	4,300	30,000	10,000	40,000

#	Name of Agency	Founded	Congr. #		Membership		Affiliate	
			1968	2000	1968	2000	1968	2000
40	Eglise Evangelique Lutherienne D'Haiti	---	---	120	---	3,500	---	12,000
41	Communion Mennonite d'Haiti	---	---	6	---	650	---	1,170
42	Petit-Anse	---	---	2	---	500	---	800

SOURCES:

Congr. stands for congregation.
* stands for roughly year 1968
** stands for roughly year 1998
--- stands for data not available

Charles-Poisset Romain, *Le Protestantisme* (Protestantism), 346.
Patrick Johnstone, *Operation World*, [CD-ROM] , 2001).

APPENDIX 6: List of Haitian Evangelical Churches in Chicago

#	Pastor	Church's Name	Address	City
1	Daniel Dumont	Première Egl. Bapt. Haitienne D'Evanston	1309 Elmwood	Evanston, IL
2	Frantz Lacombe	Nouvelle Eglise Baptiste Missionnaire	1101 Church St.	Evanston, IL
3	J. F. Valdemar	Eglise Evangelique Bethel de Chicago	1900 W. Greenleaf	Chicago, IL
4	Luckner Descorbeth Raymond Silencieux	Eglise de Dieu unifiée	7059 Grenview	Chicago, IL
5	Paul R. Bertrand	Eglise de Dieu de Broadway	5145 N. Broadway	Chicago, IL
6	Hector Mardi	New Hope Haitian Community Church	7421 N. Western Ave	Chicago, IL
7	Josué Jeanty Jean Ulysse	Eglise Baptiste de Gabaon	2805 E. 87th St.	Chicago, IL
8	Dumarsais Steide	Eglise de Dieu Du Sud	9101 S. Baltimore	Chicago, IL
9	J. O. Lilite Joseph E. Lainé Joel Metellus	Eglise Haitienne de la Grace CMA	8200 South Shore Dr.	Chicago, IL
10	Ginette Lariviere	Eglise Evang. de la Nouvelle Jérusalem	9200 S. Luella St.	Chicago, IL
11	Gerson Badette	Maranatha Mission Evangelical Church	24 N. Austin Blvd	Oak Park, IL
12	Louis D. Pierre	Assemblee Evangelique Haitienne	14226 Grant St.	Dolton, IL
13	Arthur Alexis	Eglise Bethlehem Adventiste du Jour	90th Street	Chicago, IL
14	Elie Weick	Eglise Adventiste de la Nouvelle Jerusalem	1701 W. Morse Ave	Chicago, IL

APPENDIX 7: Interviews & Communication

#	Names	Affiliation	Title	Location	Date
1	Roger/Karen See	UFM	Missionary	MI	April 13, 2000
2	Dr. Edner Jeanty	UEBH	Pastor	Haiti	April 27, 2000
3	Dr. Soliny Vedrine	EBMB/BGC	Pastor/VGPMH	Boston	June 28, 2002
4	Edner Jeanty	UEBH	Missionary	Haiti	July 27, 2002
5	Dr. Chavannes Jeune	MEBSH/WT	President	Haiti	October 5, 2002
6	Dr. Jean B. Thomas	EBEFNY/SBC	Pastor	NY	October 14, 2002
7	Dr. Jamil Georgeon	EBREF/AB	Pastor	NY	October 14, 2002
8	Dr. Jules Casséus	UCNH	President	Haiti	October 14, 2002
9	Matthieu J. Baptiste	HECA	Evangelist	Florida	October 15, 2002
10	Jean Osée Lilite	EHG	Former student STEP	Chicago	October 21, 2002
11	Dr. Fritz Fontus	ABS	Missionary Africa	Florida	October 31, 2002
12	Pierre R. Cadet	NEBM/EBM	Missionary	Haiti	December 19, 2002
13	Marie M. Eleazard	EEBB/AIM	Short-Term Missionary	Montreal	January 20, 2003
14	Rosemary Walker	AIM	Regional Coordinator	Toronto	January 21, 2003
15	Jean Wiclef Firmin	EBPA/AIM	Short Term Missionary	Montreal	January 24, 2003
16	Dr. Hebert Lacombe	Laypeople	Ph.D. Candidate	Montreal	Januray 29, 2003
17	Janette Lazer	Interact Mission	Former Missionary	WA	Januray 29, 2003
18	Edwin Walker	World Team	Retired Missionnary	USA	March 26, 2003
19	Pierre Vericain	ELBP	Short-Term Missionary	Montreal	April 3, 2003
20	Dr. Jonias Destiné	MEBSH	Short-Term Missionary	Haiti	May 3, 2003
21	Dr. Claude Noel	CEEH	Former President	Florida	July 30, 2003
22	Brezil St-Germain	MEBSH	Former President	Florida	August 13, 2003

#	Names	Affiliation	Title	Location	Date
23	Suzie Destournel	EEBB/AIM	Short-Term Missionary	Madagascar	August 13, 2003
24	Fredrine Louis	EEBB/AIM	Short-Term Missionary	Madagascar	August 13, 2003
25	Margery Berthole	FHBCO	Former Missionary	USA	10 September 2003
26	Elie D. Weick	SDA	Pastor	USA	11 September 2003
27	Roland Joachin	SDA	Professor	USA	17 September 2003
28	Pierre Deshommes	SDA	Professor	USA	17 September 2003
29	Felix Saint Louis	EBB	Pastor	USA	20 September 2003
30	George Morissette	EDO	Pastor	Canada	25 September 2003
31	Thelemaque Desamour	Baptist	Former Missionary	Canada	26 September 2003
32	Nino Amertile	SDA	Short Term Missionary	USA	2 October 2003
33	Mullery J. Pierre	BGC	Pastor	USA	2 October 2003

APPENDIX 8:
General Overview of Data Analysis

Question	#	Items								
Knowledge of GC[17]	1	**1** 18%	**2** 5%	**3** 22%	**4** 21%	**5** 35%				
5 versions of GC*	2	**1** 62%			**2** 38%					
Responsi-bility to share the gospel	3	**1** 46%			**2** 54%					
If cannot go, I would send	4	**1** 20%		**2** 21%		**3** 23%		**4** 37%		
To me "missions" is	5	**1** 63%	**2** 68%	**3** 63%	**4** 70%	**5** 56%	**6** 47%	**7** 69%	**8** 74%	**9** 21%
Feeling at ease to share my faith	6	**1** 92%			**2** 8%					
Can't make a difference in world evangel-ization	7	**1** 67%			**2** 33%					
If God would send me, I'd go to	8	**1** 10%	**2** 1%	**3** 2%	**4** 30%	**5** 54%	**6** 4%			
Activities of my church are for Haitian culture	9	**1** 49%			**2** 51%					
GC* was given to:	10	**1** 17%		**2** 42%		**3** 23%		**4** 19%		

---

[17] GC = Great Commission

Question	#	Items					
My church needs to share gospel	11	**1** 13%		**2** 86%		**3** 1%	
Outside church, I pray for missionaries	12	**1** 49%			**2** 51%		
My life reflects the GC*	13	**1** 61%			**2** 39%		
I am willing to give up if God calls me	14	**1** 10%	**2** 10%	**3** 2%	**4** 25%	**5** 39%	**6** 14%
Vision of my church is to reach Haitians	15	**1** 65%			**2** 35%		
My giving to missions has:	16	**1** 43%	**2** 32%		**3** 5%	**4** 20%	
GC* is found	17	**1** 20%	**2** 9%	**3** 3%	**4** 30%	**5** 31%	**6** 7%
My church has helped me understand the GC*	18	**1** 77%			**2** 23%		
I can't see myself reach the lost	19	**1** 27%	**2** 19%		**3** 23%	**4** 31%	
My role to fulfill the Great Commission	20	**1** 65%			**2** 35%		
If fits schedule, I'd open to cross cultural missions	21	**1** 18%	**2** 11%		**3** 33%	**4** 38%	
First heard GC sermons	22	**1** 24%	**2** 37%		**3** 22%	**4** 18%	

166

Question	#	Items								
Only missionaries have responsibility to go on the field	23	**1** 66%					**2** 34%			
Great Commission means	24	**1** 11%	**2** 32%	**3** 5%	**4** 42%	**5** 0%	**6** 11%			
First attended missions conference	25	**1** 74%					**2** 26%			
Praying at hospital is missions	26	**1** 75%					**2** 25%			
Missions of this church is to bring gospel to all nations	27	**1** 95%					**2** 5%			
Make adjustment to welcome other ethnic group	28	**1** 97%					**2** 3%			
Obeying the GC[*]	29	**1** 87%					**2** 13%			
Go anywhere is called by God	30	**1** 85%					**2** 15%			
This church more effort to nurture believers	31	**1** 55%					**2** 45%			
What I'd bring in a mission trip to Haiti	32	**1** 24%	**2** 8%	**3** 7%	**4** 13%	**5** 36%	**6** 13%			
My concern to get involved in missions	33	**1** 27%		**2** 20%		**3** 30%		**4** 24%		

Question	#	Items									
Items that are more or less motivating people to reach the lost	34		**1**	**2**	**3**	**4**	**5**	**6**	**7**	**8**	**9**
		M	48	35	38	44	38	33	29	38	34
		L	18	33	21	17	22	30	26	27	25

Question	#	Items				
Are you a Christian?	35	**1**			**2**	
		95%			5%	
How long in America?	36	**1**	**2**		**3**	**4**
		5%	12%		14%	69%
Your age?	37	**1**	**2**	**3**	**4**	**5**
		6%	32%	24%	23%	16%
Gender	38	**1**			**2**	
		36%			64%	
How long are you a Christian?	39	**1**	**2**	**3**	**4**	**5**
		35%	12%	11%	14%	27%
I attend this church	40	**1**	**2**	**3**	**4**	**5**
		48%	16%	6%	22%	8%
I was born in	41	**1**		**2**		**3**
		75%		22%		3%
I am visiting this church	42	**1**			**2**	
		56%			44%	
Language		**1**			**2**	
		38%			62%	

NOTE: All data are percentages except for question 34, which is units.

APPENDIX 9:
Evaluating Missions in the
Local Church[18]

Ten Questions Every Church should Ask

☐ **Leadership Involvement**. Do the pastor, staff, elders, and other church leaders take the lead through direction setting, personal involvement, and enthusiasm?

☐ **Heart**. Is the congregation winning people to Christ at home consistent with their desire for missionaries to win people to Christ elsewhere?

☐ **Planning**. Does the church set goals, carry them out and evaluate progress for internal mobilization and external deployment of missionaries?

☐ **Strategy**. Does the church have a direction or focus for its missions work?

☐ **Congruence**. Does the church support mission work consistent with the values and philosophy of the church's own work?

☐ **Missions Leadership Team**. Is the missions leadership team organized and effective?

☐ **Integration**. Does missions permeate the age groups, interest levels, programs, and calendar of the church?

---

[18]Used by permission: http://www.davidmays.org/Current-BN/MoreStuff.pdf (P. 46).

☐ **Congregation Participation**. Does a large portion of the congregation participate regularly by giving, praying, serving, teaching, and/or ministering?

☐ **Finances**. Is church funding for missions a large percentage of the church budget, provided for by a large percentage of the congregation well representing all adult age categories?

☐ **Relevance**. Is the church in touch with modern realities with regard to its missions work, missions image, communication methods, and partnering and networking?

APPENDIX 10:
Steps to Start a Missions Ministry in Your Church[19]

Pray
- ☐ Pray for your church and your pastor daily.
- ☐ Recruit others to pray with you.
- ☐ Pray and talk positively.

Get Personally Involved in Missions
- ☐ Find missions stuff to read.
- ☐ Develop a relationship with a missionary.
- ☐ Begin giving to missions.

Volunteer to Help Your Pastor
- ☐ Find out the pastor's interests in missions.
- ☐ See what the pastor would like done.
- ☐ Offer to organize a missions team or task force.

Investigate What's Already Going On
- ☐ Find out who is interested in missions.
- ☐ Learn what your church and denomination are already doing.
- ☐ Learn what missionaries and organizations people already know.

Assemble A Missions Team Or Task Force
- ☐ Agree to meet regularly.
- ☐ Review the status and consider possibilities for missions in the church.
- ☐ Develop a preliminary organizational structure.

Educate the Team in Missions
- ☐ Obtain and study some good resources.
- ☐ Attend an ACMC Conference and take the Perspectives Course.
- ☐ Invite a missions pastor from a strong missions church to consult with the group.

---

[19]Used by permission: http://www.davidmays.org/Current-BN/MoreStuff.pdf (P. 39).

Investigate Missions Opportunities
☐ Find out what missionaries supported by the church (or by individuals) are doing.
☐ Investigate what your denomination is currently pushing.
☐ Consider what minorities are in your community.

Communicate Missions to the Church
☐ Do a missions conference.
☐ Bring in missionaries to give reports.
☐ Include missions information in the weekly bulletin.

Engage in Mission Efforts
☐ Begin supporting missionaries.
☐ Send groups on short-term trips.
☐ Begin to reach out to people of other cultures nearby.

APPENDIX 11:
Issues in Communicating Missions to the Local Church[20]

☐ Promotion – Advertising
- Getting people's attention
- Developing enthusiasm

☐ Awareness – Letting people know what is going on
- How the world is changing
- What God is doing
- Where Christians are hurting
- Where Christianity is progressing
- What the great needs and barriers are
- What our denomination, agencies and missionaries are doing
- What new strategies and avenues of ministry are

☐ Education – The basics of missions
- Biblical instruction
- Missions history and missionary heroes of the past
- Global status and recent big changes
- Geography, peoples and countries
- Strategies
- Culture

☐ Intensive and Extensive Communication – Providing for in-depth exposure and also keeping missions in view everywhere

☐ Missions Events – Doing conferences, special emphases and activities

☐ The Profile of Missions - Giving missions a high level of visibility in the church

☐ The Image of Missions – Giving missions a contemporary, relevant, significant look

---

[20] Used by permission: http://www.davidmays.org/Current-BN/MoreStuff.pdf (P. 50).

- ☐ Presenting Missions in Contemporary Services
- ☐ Communicating Missions through Worship
- ☐ Integrating Missions – Making missions a natural part of every ministry, age group, and interest level
- ☐ Communicating across Generations
- ☐ Becoming Aware of attitudes, feelings, experience, and knowledge about missions
- ☐ Contextualizing - Helping missionaries and missions speakers communicate effectively to our people.

APPENDIX 12:
STEPS TO A GOOD
MISSIONS CONFERENCE[21]

The keys to a good missions conference are **purpose**, **prayer**, **planning**, **promotion**, **program**, and **follow up**.

☐ Select the date and make sure it doesn't conflict with anything that will compete for a large section of your congregation. Set the date well in advance, up to one year.

☐ Recruit a respected and effective leader to head up the Conference Team. Assemble a separate conference leadership team. Include lots of people in the planning and preparation.

☐ Plan well in advance, at least six months.

☐ Pray before you do anything else, while you are doing everything else, and after everything is done. Prayer is perhaps the single most important part of the Conference.

☐ Develop a purpose for the conference. What do you hope to accomplish?

☐ Find the best keynote speaker you can get. The missions speaker sets the tone.

☐ Develop a solid program with elements of creativity, drama, storytelling, and lots of participation. Do at least one new thing you haven't done before.

☐ Do a special education effort for church leaders.

---

[21] Used by permission: http://www.davidmays.org/Current-BN/MoreStuff.pdf (P. 56).

175

☐ Run a children's conference at the same time.

☐ Make your promotion as good as the best event in your church.

☐ Showcase your missionaries to their best advantage.

☐ Call people to commitment. Challenge big. Give them several alternatives for response. Provide a way for them to record their response. Provide ways to begin implementing their commitments immediately.

☐ Follow up on the responses and help people to carry out their commitments.

APPENDIX 13:
Issues for a Short-Term Missions Policy[22]

Definition: What constitutes a short-term mission?

Goals: What do you want to accomplish with short-term missions?

Application Procedures: How does someone get approved?

Criteria for Selection:

☐ How do you decide whether an individual is eligible?

☐ What sponsoring organizations are eligible?

☐ What types of ministry or activity are eligible? What are the priorities?

Expectations:

☐ What preparation is expected? How much notice is required?

☐ What is expected from the short-termer on-site?

☐ What reporting and follow-up is expected after the short-term?

Finances: How will short-term trips be financed?

☐ What kind of fund-raising will be allowed? Required?

☐ Will individuals be required, encouraged, or allowed to contribute to their own support?

☐ What qualifies for support from the church budget and how much is provided?

☐ Will church sponsored trips be financed differently from other trips?

---

[22] Used by permission: http://www.davidmays.org/Current-BN/MoreStuff.pdf (P. 64).

☐ Will additional church funding be considered for church staff or trip leaders?

Types of Trips: What types of trips will be considered? Which have priority?

☐ An individual applying to go with an organization for a trip or a summer

☐ An individual going for a business or medical internship

☐ A missionary candidate taking a trip as part of training or investigating a field

☐ Groups taking a trip

☐ Individuals or groups going on a "vacation with a purpose."

☐ Church staff taking a vision trip or a trip to encourage missionaries or to explore fields.

APPENDIX 14:
The Pastor's Roles in Missions[23]

Student. Study the theme of missions in Scripture and missions books.
God's glory in all the earth may be considered the unifying theme of Scripture. Study the Scripture through the big picture lens of God's heart for all peoples.

Model. Set the pace for personal involvement.
Establish and maintain missions education and involvement in your
  – reading and study
  – personal worship and prayer
  – awareness of world events
  – ongoing education experiences such as missions conferences and seminars
  – maintaining contact and praying for one or more missionaries
  – occasional visits to a missions project or ministry

Leader. Establish how world evangelism fits in the purpose of your church.
All worship, all discipleship, and all outreach – in effect, all ministries - may be undertaken for the larger purpose that Christ be known and worshipped in all the earth.
Write or rewrite the church purpose statement to give world evangelization a prominent or central focus.

Motivator. Be a spokesperson for missions.
Pray for a missionary, people, country, or world event in every service.
Preach missions where you find it in the Scripture.

---

[23] Used by permission: http://www.davidmays.org/Current-BN/MoreStuff.pdf (P. 24).

Use missionary and cross-cultural illustrations.

Introduce, promote and support missions events, projects and activities.

Bring in outside speakers to reinforce the missionary message.

Mobilizer. Observe gifts and encourage Kingdom service.

Disciple church leaders in God's worldwide purpose. Mentor a few.

Help leaders see where missions fits in their ministries and programs.

Encourage those with God's calling to missions service.

Researcher and Strategist. Take advantage of available resources.

Keep your congregation up-to-date regarding world trends and what God is doing.

Help your missions team discern the most valuable and strategic missions ministries.

APPENDIX 15:
Principles for Influencing Individuals for Missions[24]

☐ **Modeling**: What you are teaches more than what you say.

☐ **Relationships**: People buy into you and then your vision.

☐ **Prayer**: God can move people by prayer alone.

☐ **Care**: People respond when you take an interest in them.

☐ **Exposure**: People are moved by exposure to missionaries and seeing God at work.

☐ **Experience**: Spectators become critics. Participants become boosters.

☐ **Mission Trips**: Being told is boring. Finding out is exciting.

☐ **New Believers**: They are quick to understand.

☐ **Conferences**: Enthusiasm is contagious.

☐ **Recruit**: Watch and pray for someone to help you.

☐ **Challenge**: Challenge to a special assignment.

☐ **Niches**: Help people find their special niche.

☐ **Children**: People are influenced by their children – and vice versa, of course.

☐ **Patience**: Kingdom work is slow.

☐ **Surprise**: You influence people unknowingly.

---

[24] Used by permission: http://www.davidmays.org/Current-BN/MoreStuff.pdf (P. 39).

- ☐ **Multiplication**: God may use someone you influence to influence many others.

- ☐ **You are not alone:** God also uses other people, events, and circumstances.

- ☐ **The First Rule:** Do whatever you can as well as you can wherever you are with whatever you have.

- ☐ **Authenticity**: We can only take people where we have been ourselves.

- ☐ **Attitude**: They will only want to go with you if they like you. Attitude is everything!

APPENDIX 16:
Biblical Stewardship

Teaching

This section provides internet references for stewardship. The teaching presented in this site reflects the Evangelical doctrines of stewardship.

1. The Biblical Case for Giving.
http://www.generousgiving.org/page.asp?sec=28&page=63

2. What the Bible says about Money and Giving.
http://www.generousgiving.org/page.asp?sec=9&page

3. The Teaching of Generosity
http://www.generousgiving.org/page.asp?sec=28&page=64

4. The Church and Its Money
http://www.generousgiving.org/page.asp?sec=28&page=62
http://www.generousgiving.org/page.asp?sec=81&page=#Stott
1 http://www.generousgiving.org/page.asp?sec=50&page=84
http://www.generousgiving.org/page.asp?sec=50&page=83
http://www.generousgiving.org/page.asp?sec=50&page=85
http://www.generousgiving.org/page.asp?sec=50&page=175

Books

The following books are recommended for any serious Biblical study on stewardship.

Biblical Stewardship by Alfred Martin: Loizeaux Brothers; Rev. Edition, 1991.

Neither Poverty nor Riches by Craig Bloomberg: Intervarsity Press, 2001

APPENDIX 17:
How to Help Your Pastor in
Missions[25]

☐ Provide him with prayer resources.

☐ Pray for him regularly.

☐ Send him to the mission field.

☐ Arrange for missionaries to visit him.

☐ Pay his way to a conference or class such as ACMC[26], Urbana, Perspectives

☐ Enlist the pastor's participation in the missions conference and committee.

☐ Provide helpful missions reading material, such as
- Clipped articles and illustrations
- *Eternity in Their Hearts*
- *Key to the Missionary Problem*
- *Get Your Church Involved in Missions*
- *Let the Nations Be Glad*

☐ Handle the details of missions.

☐ Make sure your pastor is "the hero."

☐ Be willing to suggest and implement your good ideas.

☐ Work with the pastor and board to define missions.

☐ Suggest new options for increasing missions giving.

☐ Encourage her to talk with other missions-minded pastors.

☐ Support and affirm his ideas for missions.

Tips...

☐ Don't become a pest to be avoided.

☐ Demonstrate genuine interest and involvement in other church ministries.

---

[25] Used by permission: http://www.davidmays.org/Current-BN/MoreStuff.pdf (P. 22).

[26] Advancing Churches in Missions Commitment

☐ Be patient and go slowly.
☐ Don't criticize.
☐ Seek and receive permission and endorsement of all missions activities.
☐ Ask the pastor to personally promote missions publicly.
☐ Do everything for missions in a quality manner.
☐ Don't lose heart and try to work around the pastor.
☐ Affirm everything the pastor does for missions.

APPENDIX 18:
Sermon Outline

Text: Mark 16:14-16
Title: Into all the World

Introduction:

Secular: Christopher Columbus's vision to conquer a new world.

Personal: Ask a few questions

Biblical: God is interested in the world that He created and all the people who live in it. He is concerned about restoring the broken relationships with all the people on the face of the earth.

Textual: Mark 16:14-16

Transition:

Setting: Post-resurrection of Jesus Christ

Issues: Textual critic (long and short ending of Mark)

Jesus gave instructions to His disciples in 3 areas:

I. Motivation (v.14)

What should motivate the believer/church to go into the world? It is the condition of mankind on the face of the globe. Man's spiritual condition in the universe is: depraved, alienated, in bondage, broken relationships, loneliness, in a state of guilt, shame, fear, wickedness, hopeless and helpless, needs to belong, searching, ignorance, insecurity, darkness - a world full of trouble. It is a global problem touching every country on the face of the earth which calls for a worldwide mission with a universal solution. God is zeroing on the world with the vision to meet its needs through the person of Jesus Christ. He tells His church where to go and what to do. Therefore, the church has been called to a global task

A. Illustration: Dwight L. Moody's motivation to daily share the Gospel.

B. Application:

- How does that look like for the believers of any nations

- How can the Haitian church be motivated to share the gospel?

- What can the Haitian Pastor do to motivate His congregation?

Transition: Since God is motivated to bring a solution to the world, believers should be motivated to do the same. This leads to the second area of instruction.

I. Responsibility (v.15)

- To respond to man's global problem, God gives one universal solution which is the preaching of the Gospel of Jesus Christ.

- What is the Gospel? It is the good news about the death and resurrection of Jesus Christ. The believer at all times is responsible to get that message out.

- **It is a matter of obedience to Jesus' command, not an option**: To go and to preach the good news to the whole creation (v.15).

A. It is a matter of priority for the church: The church has one priority – to get the good news out in every language of the world, to all ethnic group on the face of the earth (v.15)

B. It is a matter of accountability. The believer will give an account to God for the way He (she) carries out that command (v.15)

C. It is a matter of involvement. Believer as churches can be involved in all kind of ways: Prayer, giving, translating, health care, as a lawyer, an engineer, accountant, professor, camp ministry, whatever gifts or talents can be used for that purpose (v.15)

1. Illustration: William Carey who went to India

2. Application:

   - How can the Haitian church take responsibility for the Great Commission?

   - Activities to share the Gospel with the youth, adult, Pastors, family?

   - Secure a budget for missions in the local church

   - Financially support a missionary in another country than home?

Transition: Since God is motivated to bring a solution to the world and entrusted to us the responsibility to proclaim the message, believers should be assured about the outcome. This leads to the third area of instruction.

III. Outcome (v.16)

A. Those who accept the Gospel will be saved (v.16a)

B. Those who reject the Gospel will be condemned (v.16b)

    1. Illustration: The story of Saint Augustine's conversion

    2. Application:

        - How can one shares the good news in their immediate community?

        - Among the wealthy, the middle class, neighbor, co-worker…?

Transition: God wants the church to be motivated, take responsibility to bring the message to the world and the outcome is certain.

Conclusion. Having heard God's word zeroing in on the vision to reach a dying and desperate world, how is the believer to respond? He/she needs to respond by getting motivated, taking on his/her responsibility because the outcome is certain whether the message is received or rejected.

APPENDIX 19:
Keys for Missions Committee Operation[27]

☐ **Define your task**
   Define missions for your church.
   Draw your boundaries
   Determine your responsibilities

☐ **Determine what qualities and skills you need**
   Pray for what you need
   Watch for individuals with the right qualities
   Recruit them

☐ **Keep learning and growing**
   Find out how you learn best
   Identify appropriate resources and tools
   Hold yourselves accountable

☐ **Build Community**
   Get to know one another
   Communicate frequently
   Pray for one another
   Have fun

☐ **Model missions for the congregation**
   Do missions yourselves
   Learn and pray
   Give generously

☐ **Divide up the work for task teams**
   Determine the teams you need
   Find a good leader who has a passion for the area
   Help the leader lay out a plan

☐ **Develop and use good policies and procedures**
   Find out what policies you already have

---

[27] Used by permission: http://www.davidmays.org/Current-BN/MoreStuff.pdf (P. 18).

Get input from church leaders and others
Approve and use the policy by sections

APPENDIX 20:
The Job of the Missions Committee[28]

GENERAL FUNCTIONS

☐ Make Policy Decisions/Recommendations
☐ Establish Organization
☐ Plot Strategy
☐ Evaluate Finances

SPECIFIC TASKS

☐ Missions Policy
☐ Missions Communication
☐ Raise Finances
☐ Administer Finances
☐ Prayer/Correspondence
☐ Annual Missions Event
☐ Missions Education
☐ Care for Missionaries
☐ Missionary Recruitment
☐ Liaison with Missions Agencies
☐ Short Term Trips
☐ Missionary Preparation

GOAL STATEMENTS

☐ Purpose: What is Our Job?
☐ Long Range: More than One Year
☐ Short Range: Less than One Year

---

[28] Used by permission: http://www.davidmays.org/Current-BN/MoreStuff.pdf (P. 15).

APPENDIX 21:
Steps for a Missions Planning Retreat[29]

☐ Set aside a time, perhaps a one-day retreat.

☐ Employ a facilitator.

☐ Identify the functions or areas for planning.

☐ Brainstorm possible futures.

☐ Identify the person primarily responsible for each function.

☐ Divide into subgroups around each function.

☐ Each subgroup write a purpose statement for their function.

☐ Each subgroup write one or more goals.
- Long term goals require more than one year.
- Short term goals require less than one year.

☐ Submit the goals to the committee chairperson or designate who will edit the goals for goal criteria and style consistency.

☐ Each subgroup approve the final draft and distribute the goals to all members.

☐ Follow up on goal progress at each regular meeting.

Smart Goals[30]:

S	Specific	Only one thing.
M	Measurable	You know when it's done.
A	Accountable	You know who is to do it.
R	Reachable	It is possible.
T	Time	You know when it is supposed to be done.

---

[29] Used by permission: http://www.davidmays.org/Current-BN/MoreStuff.pdf (P. 39).

[30] Source: "Organizing and Leading Your Missions Committee," by Doug Christgau.

APPENDIX 22:
Missions Management Basics[31]

☐ **Why do we do it? (purpose or mission)**

This is the question of purpose. The missions team answers this question in two ways:

1. "Why do we exist?" That is, "Why does this missions team exist?"

In its essence, the missions team exists to help church leaders carry out the missions aspect of the church's purpose.

2. "Why do we do missions?" That is, "Why does our church do missions?"

This question is answered biblically and the answer may develop or spell out what is suggested in the church constitution or purpose statement.

☐ **What is missions? (definition or boundaries)**

The definition establishes the boundaries. Missions committees may find themselves dealing with and funding too many ministries of too broad a scope. Missions becomes miscellaneous. In order to clarify what qualifies for missions funding and to limit the workload, it is valuable to draw boundaries.

For your church, does missions include?

Ministry outside the U.S. only   or some ministries inside the U.S. as well?

Cross-cultural ministry only or some same culture ministry as well?

Evangelism & church planting only or relief, development, & support ministries, as well?

---

[31] Used by permission: http://www.davidmays.org/ Current-BN/MoreStuff.pdf (P. 34).

Field ministry only or administration and support as well?

Spiritual ministry only or social ministry as well?

Social ministry with clear spiritual aims only or social ministry for its own sake as well?

Missionary support only or projects and organizations as well?

Missionaries from your church or denomination only or other missionaries as well?

Vocational ministry only or short-term missions and mission trips as well?

Ministry done only by those sent or work done by the congregation as well?

American missionaries only or partnership with nationals as well?

Work done outside the church only or work done by your church on your premises as well?

☐ **Where are we headed? (vision or strategy)**

Vision and strategy are two quite different things but they both give direction and focus to the missions ministry. They help us decide what to give preference and priority. Vision is a clear, detailed mental picture of a future we hope to achieve. It is narrow, specific, and focused. Strategy is a general direction to pursue, a hierarchy of priorities.

☐ **How do we do it? (policies and procedures)**

Policies and procedures help us organize ourselves and conduct our business in an orderly and systematic manner. The "missions policy" is an overall document that includes the above philosophical issues as well as the structure, operation, and job descriptions of the missions leadership team as well as guidelines for how missions is conducted and missions income is generated, budgeted and spent.

APPENDIX 23: HAITIAN MISSIONARIES WHO MINISTERED OVERSEAS

#	Missionary Name & Hometown	Country	Church	Denomi-nation	Haitian Support	Agency	Yr. of Depar-ture	Main Responsibility	Yrs. Of Service [32]
1	Fritz Fontus (FL)	USA	---	Baptist	0%	ABS/ UBA	1965	Teaching	14 ½
2	Rolland Joachin (CA)	France	---	Adventist	SDA	SDA	1967	Teaching	29
3	Felix Saint-Louis (FL)	Haiti	MEBSH	Baptist	MEBSH	MEBSH	1969	Planter	11
4	Eugene Germain (N/A)	Haiti	---	Pentecostal	N/A	ED	1969?	Missionary	N/A
5	George Morissette (Montréal)	Canada	EDO	Pentecostal	Various	ED	1970	Teaching	Various
6	Michel Cherenfant (Haiti)	Haiti	---	Adventist	SDA	SDA	1972	Teaching	12
7	Joses L. Joseph (N/A)	Canada	---	Adventist	SDA	SDA	1976	Teaching	12
8	Marie Lourdes Noel (MA)	Boston	EDB	Pentecostal	N/A	ED	N/A	Teaching	Various
9	Télémaque/ A Desamour (ON)	Canada	AIM	Baptist	0%	AIM	1977	Medical	2
10	Simon et Suzanne Honoré (MI)	Haiti	---	Adventist	SDA	SDA	1980	Teaching	6
11	Pierre Deshommes (MA)	Canada	---	Adventist	SDA	SDA	1983	Administrator	8
12	Alcega Janiton (N/A)	Haiti	---	Adventist	SDA	SDA	N/A	Director	12
13	Disciple et Nino Amertil (MA)	USA	---	Adventist	SDA	SDA	1984	Director	3

[32] For specific information on the actual fields of mission work for each missionary, see chapter 2.

#	Missionary Name & Hometown	Country	Church	Denomi-nation	Haitian Support	Agency	Yr. of Depar-ture	Main Responsibility	Yrs. Of Service [32]
14	Max Jose Pierre (NY)	Haiti	----	Adventist	SDA	SDA	1986	Teaching	12
15	Marc Hancy St-Charles (PAP)	Haiti	EBT/UEBH	Baptist	80%	OM	1989	Evangelism	4
16	Myrtha Eleazard (Montreal)	Canada	EEBB	Baptist	0%	AIM	1990	Evangelism	3 mos.
17	Edner/Dominique Jeanty (PAP)	Haiti	EBB/EBT	Baptist	50%	UFM	1995	Teaching	1 1/2
18	Jonias Destiné (PAP)	Haiti	Cote Plage	Baptist	0%	LMM	1997	Medical care	6 wks.
19	Ronald Jean Louis (PAP)	Haiti	Mon Joli	Baptist	0%	LMM	1997	Medical care	6 wks.
20	Adelson Jean Simon (Bonne fin)	Haiti	Bonne-fin	Baptist	0%	LMM	1997	Medical care	6 wks.
21	Nanette Desvarennes (Bonnefin)	Haiti	Bonne-fin	Baptist	0%	LMM	1997	Medical care	6 wks.
22	Jean W. Firmin (Montréal)	Canada	EBPA	Baptist	100 % *	AIM	2000	Teaching	3 mos.
23	Margery Berthole (Orlando)	USA	FHBCO	Baptist	30%	Student	2000	Teaching	2 wks.
24	Pierre Vericain (Montréal)	Canada	LBP	Protestant	Self	LBP	2002	Teaching	3 wks.
25	Pierre & Yvette Cadet (Chicago)	Haiti	EHMN	Baptist	15%	EBM	2003	Teaching	3 wks.
26	Fredrine Louis (Montreal)	Canada	EEBB	Baptist	67%	AIM	2003	Teaching	3 mos.

#	Missionary Name & Hometown	Country	Church	Denomi-nation	Haitian Support	Agency	Yr. of Depar-ture	Main Responsibility	Yrs. Of Service [32]
27	Suzie Destournel (Montreal)	Canada	EEBB	Baptist	67%	AIM	2003	Teaching	3 mos.

APPENDIX 24: POPULATION GROWTH IN HAITI, 1824 – 2025 (IN MILLIONS)

Sources	1824	1850	1900	1920	1980	2000	2003	2005	2010	2025
Pop. Bul.[33]	-----	.9	1.3	-----	5.5	8.4	-----	-----	-----	-----
Romain[34]	.7	-----	-----	2.1	5.9	-----	-----	-----	-----	-----
PRB[35]	-----	-----	-----	-----	-----	-----	-----	-----	-----	9.6
UN[36]	-----	-----	-----	-----	5.4	8.3	-----	9.1	9.9	12.5
O. World[37]	-----	-----	-----	2.0	5.4	8.2	-----	8.9	9.6	11.9
W. Bank[38]	-----	-----	-----	-----	-----	8.0	-----	-----	-----	-----

[33] Jorge A. Brea, "Population Dynamics in Latin America," Population Bulletin, Vol. 58, no. 1 (March 2003): 7.

[34] Charles-Poisset Romain, *Le Protestantisme Dans La Société Haïtienne: Contribution à l'étude d'une religion* (Protestantism in the Haitian Society : Contribution to the study of a religion), (Port-Au-Prince: Imprimerie Henri Deschamps, 1986), 90, 96.

[35] http://www.prb.org/pdf/WorldPopulationDS02_Eng.pdf (Population Reference Bureau)

[36] http://www.eclac.org/publicaciones/Estadisticas/8/LCG2118PB/c-2-I.pdf (United Nation Statistics)

[37] Patrick Johnstone, *Operation World, English Full-Text Database Software*, [CD-ROM] (Waynesboro, GA: Paternoster-publishing, 2001).

[38] http://devdata.worldbank.org/external/CPProfile.asp?CCODE=HTI&PTYPE=CP (World Bank)

Sources	1824	1850	1900	1920	1980	2000	2003	2005	2010	2025
IHSI[39]	-----	-----	-----	-----	-----	-----	-----	-----	-----	13.1
Estimate[40]	-----	-----	-----	-----	-----	-----	8.5	-----	-----	-----

[39] http://www.haitimedical.com/haiti_stats.htm (Institut Haitien de Statistique et d'informatique ; Haitian Institute of statistics and information)

[40] Based on the overall data presented on this chart, the author estimated the Haitian population in 2003 to 8.5 million.

APPENDIX 25:
CONGREGATIONAL SURVEY

Thank you in advance for participating in this important survey. We ask you to be honest and open in how you answer these questions. Your name does not appear anywhere on this questionnaire, and all your answers will be confidential. Unless otherwise noted, please respond with only one best or most correct answer for each question. The survey should take you about 9 to 13 minutes to complete.

1) In my opinion, my knowledge of the Great Commission is:
(Circle a number along this scale)
              1 2 3 4 5
     Weak   Strong

2) To me Jesus' followers reported 5 versions of the Great Commission in the New Testament __Yes __No

3) I feel God gives to only a few people in the church the responsibility to share the Gospel with people who have not heard it.
_____ Agree _____ Disagree

4) If I cannot go wherever as a missionary, I would send? (Check one)
___My Spouse ____My Children ____My best friend _____ Nobody

5) To me, "missions" is: (check all that you feel describe missions)
- ❑ Reaching the lost primarily overseas
- ❑ Visiting people at the hospital
- ❑ Helping the poor
- ❑ Sharing the Gospel with prisoners in Jail
- ❑ Reaching Haitians primarily with the Gospel
- ❑ Primarily the job of missionaries
- ❑ The responsibility of every church, including ours
- ❑ The responsibility of every believer, including me
- ❑ Something else

6) I feel at ease sharing my faith with others ___ Yes ___ No

7) World evangelization is such a huge task I ask myself, what difference can I make? __Agree __Disagree

8) If God would send me as a missionary, I would go to? (Check one)
___Canada ____Russia ____China ___Haiti ___Anywhere
_____Nowhere

9) For me the activities of my church are designed primarily for Haitian culture
___ Yes ___No

10) To me, the Great Commission was given? (Check one)
a. _____To the 12 disciples alone
b. _____To all the disciples of Jesus Christ
c. _____To every human being
d. _____Don't know

11) I feel that my church needs to share the Gospels with? (Check one)
a. ___Haitians   b. ___Everybody   c. ___Don't know

12) In my prayer time (outside the church), I have prayed for missionaries
regularly ___ Yes ___ No

13) The way I live my life now reflects the mandate of the Great Commission
_____ Yes _____No

14) If God would call me as a missionary, I am willing to give up? (Check one)
___ My job ___ My school ___ My church __Anything __ All ___ Nothing

15) The vision of my church according to the Bible should be to reach all
Haitians for Christ__ Yes ___No

16) Over the past year my giving to missions has (check one)
   ❑   Increased
   ❑   Remained the same
   ❑   Gone down
   ❑   Not applicable (I don't give for missions)

17) For me the Great Commission is found: (Check one)
a. ___ In the Gospels alone
b. ___ In Matthew alone
c. ___ In Acts alone
d. ___ In the Gospels and Acts
e. ___ In the Old Testament
f. ___ Don't know

18) I feel what I have learned in my church has helped me understand the Great
Commission __ Yes __ No

19) Reaching the lost for Christ is important, but I can't see myself doing it. (Check one)
- ❑ Strongly disagree
- ❑ Somewhat disagree
- ❑ Strongly agree
- ❑ Somewhat agree

20) I have a very clear idea of what my role is in helping fulfill the Great Commission __Agree __Disagree

21) If it fits my schedule, I would be open to a short-term, cross-cultural mission experience (Check one)
- ❑ Strongly disagree
- ❑ Somewhat disagree
- ❑ Somewhat agree
- ❑ Strongly agree

22) For me, I have first heard sermons on the Great Commission (Check one)
- ❑ In Haiti
- ❑ In this church
- ❑ Nowhere
- ❑ In this place (_____)

23) I feel that only the missionaries have the responsibility to go on the field:
___ Yes ___ No

24) In my opinion, the Great Commission means? (Check one)
- ❑ Evangelize specially the Haitians
- ❑ Preach the Gospel to Haitians and all the people on earth
- ❑ Visit people at hospital
- ❑ Make disciples and preach the Gospel to all nations
- ❑ Organize missions trip primarily to Haiti
- ❑ Supporting missionaries if I cannot go

25) For me, I first attended missions conference in Haiti
___ Yes ___ No

26) I would consider praying with someone at the hospital, as equivalent to missions _ Yes _ No

27) For me, the mission of this church is to bring the Gospels to all the nations of the earth ___ Yes ___No

28) I am willing to make adjustment to welcome other nationalities in my church
___ Yes ___ No

29) I am willing to obey the Great Commission no matter the cost
_____ Yes _____ No

30) I am planning to go anywhere if God would call me as a missionary ___ Yes
___ No (Check one)

31) This church should focus more effort on nurturing believers who attend here and less on changing the world ___ Yes ___ No

32) The most important thing I would bring in a mission trip in Haiti is (Check one)
- ❑ Medication
- ❑ Food
- ❑ Clothes
- ❑ Money
- ❑ Bible
- ❑ _____

33) I would like to get involved in missions, but my concern is: (check one)
a. ____ Fear
b. ____ Language
c. ____ Finance
d. _____ other

34) Here is a list of items which could motivate people to be more committed to reaching the lost people. Choose **four items** with "M" for what is most motivating to you, and **four items** with "L" for what is less motivating to you.
_____ Missions conference
_____ Pastor's sermon
_____ Missions reports in our church services
_____ Missionary guest speakers in Sunday services
_____ A missionary visiting me in my home
_____ Prayer letters from missionaries
_____ Attending seminars on missions
_____ Videos to help me better understand mission issues on the field.
_____ Attending Bible study on the Great Commission

35) Are you a Christian? ___ Yes ___ No

36) How long have you been in America? (Check one)
- ☐ Less than a year
- ☐ 1 - 4 years
- ☐ 5 – 10 years
- ☐ More than 10 years

37) What is your age? (Check one)
- ☐ Below 12
- ☐ 13 – 25
- ☐ 26 – 38
- ☐ 39 – 51
- ☐ 52 and more.

38) Gender: ___ Male ___Female (Check one)

39) I have been a Christian for (years)
___0-5 ___6-10 ___11-15 ___16-21 ___ 22 and + (Check one)

40) I attend this church
__ Weekly ___ Bi-weekly___ Monthly __ Occasionally __ First time (Check one)

41) I was born in
____Haiti
____Unites States of America
_____Elsewhere
(Check one)

42) I am visiting this church ____Yes _____ No, and my home church is:
_____

That's it. Thank you so much for your cooperation!

APPENDIX 26:
SONDAGE DE LA CONGREGATION – FRANÇAIS

Merci d'avance de votre participation à ce sondage important. Nous vous demandons d'être honnête et ouvert dans la façon dont vous répondez à ces questions. Votre nom n'apparaît pas sur ce questionnaire, et toutes vos réponses seront confidentielles. A défaut de note, veuillez répondre à chaque question par la meilleure réponse ou celle la plus exacte. Ce sondage prendra environ 9 à 13 minutes pour le compléter.

1) Selon mon opinion, ma connaissance de la Grande Commission est:
(Encercler un numéro)
       1 2 3 4 5
    Faible   Forte

2) D'après moi, les disciples de Jésus ont reporté 5 versions de la Grande Commission dans le Nouveau Testament __Oui __Non

3) Je sens que Dieu donne à quelques personnes dans l'église la responsabilité de partager l'évangile avec les gens qui ne l'ont pas entendues.
____ d'acccord ____ Désaccord

4) Si je ne peux pas aller n'importe où comme un missionaire, Je pourrais envoyer: (Choisir une réponse)
____Mon époux (se)
____Mes enfants
____Mon meilleur ami (e)
____ Personne

5) Pour moi, "la mission" est: (choisir tout ce que décrit la mission)
- ❑ Rejoindre les perdus principalement à l'étranger
- ❑ Visiter les gens à l'hopital
- ❑ Aider les pauvres
- ❑ Partager l'évangile avec les prisonniers à la prison
- ❑ Rejoindre les Haitiens principalement par l'évangile
- ❑ Principalement le travail des missionnaires
- ❑ La responsabilité de chaque église, inclus la nôtre
- ❑ La responsabilité de chaque chrétien, inclus moi-même
- ❑ Quelque chose d'autre

6) Je me sens à l'aise de partager ma foi avec les autres
___ Oui ___ Non

7) L'évangélisation du monde est une tâche énorme. Je me demande quelle différence je puisse faire__D'accord__Désaccord

8) Si Dieu m'envoyait comme un missionnaire, je pourrais aller (choisir une réponse)
___Canada ____Russie ____Chine ___Haiti ___N'importe où
____ Pas maintenant

9) Pour moi, les activités de mon église sont désignées principalement pour la culture Haitienne _Oui_Non

10) Pour moi, la Grande Commission était donnée (Choisir une réponse)
a. ____Aux 12 disciples Seulement
b. ____A tous les disciples de Jésus Christ
c. ____A tous les êtres humains
d. ____ Je ne sais pas

11) Je sens que mon église a besoin de partager l'évangile avec
a. ___Les Haitiens   b. ___Tout le monde   c. ___Je ne sais pas

12) Dans ma prière (à l'extérieur de l'église), je prie régulièrement pour les missionnaires ___Oui __ Non

13) La facon dont je vis maintenant reflète le mandat de la Grande Commission
____ Oui ____Non

14) Si Dieu m'appelerait comme un missionnaire, je suis disposé à abandoner (Choisir une réponse)
___ Mon travail ___ Mon école ___ Mon église __N'importe quoi __ Tout
___ Rien

15) La vision de mon église devrait atteindre tous les Haitiens en Christ
___ Oui ___Non

16) Depuis l'année dernière ma contribution pour la mission (choisir une réponse)
- ❑   a augmenté
- ❑   est restée la même
- ❑   a diminué
- ❑   Non applicable (Je ne contribue pas pour la mission)

17) Pour moi la Grande Commission se retrouve: (Choisir une reponse)
a. ___Dans les évangiles seulement
b. ___Dans Matthieu Seulement
c. ___Dans Acts Seulement
d. ___Dans les évangiles et Actes
e. ___Dans l'Ancien Testament
f. ___Je ne sais pas

18) Ce que j'ai appris à cette église semble m'aider à comprendre la Grande Commission _ Oui__ Non

19) Rejoindre les perdus pour Christ est important, mais je ne me vois pas accomplir cette tache
❑ Grandement en désaccord
❑ Un peu en déesaccord
❑ Un peu en accord
❑ Grandement en accord

20) J'ai une idée claire de mon rôle à aider à accomplir la Grande Commission
___ Accord ___ Désaccord

21) Si cela me convient, je serais ouvert à participer a une expérience missionnaire dans une culture différente
❑ Grandement en désaccord
❑ Un peu en désaccord
❑ Un peu en accord
❑ Grandement en accord

22) Pour moi, j'ai entendu pour la première fois un sermon sur la Grande Commission (choisir une réponse)
❑ En Haiti
❑ A mon église
❑ Nulle part
❑ A cette place (_____)

23) Je sens que seulement les missionnaires ont la responsabilité d'aller en mission: ___Oui ___ Non

24) Selon mon opinion, la Grande Commission veut dire (choisir une réponse)
❑ Evangeliser spécialement les Haitiens
❑ Prêcher l'évangile aux Haitiens et à tout le monde sur la terre
❑ Visiter les gens a l'hopital
❑ Faire des disciples et prêcher l'évangile a toutes les nations
❑ Organiser un voyage missionnaire principalement en Haiti
❑ Supporter les missionnaires si je ne peux pas aller

25) Pour moi, j'ai assisté pour la première fois à une conférence missionnaire en Haiti ___Oui ___ Non

26) Je considérerais prier avec quelqu'un à l'hôpital comme équivalent à la mission _ Oui _ Non

27) Pour moi, la mission de cette église est d'évangéliser toutes les nations de la terre _ Oui__Non

28) Je suis disposé à faire des ajustements afin d'accueillir autres nationalités à mon église __ Oui ___Non

29) Je suis disposé à obéir à la Grande Commission quelque soit le coût ____ Oui ____ Non ____

30) Je suis disponible d'aller n'importe ou si Dieu m'appellerait comme un missionnaire ___ Oui ___ Non

31) Cette église devrait se concentrer à nourrir les chrétiens qui y sont et moins à changer le monde ___Oui ___Non

32) La plus importante que je voudrais apporter dans un voyage missionnaire en Haiti est (choisir une)
- ❑ Medicaments
- ❑ Nourriture
- ❑ Habits
- ❑ Argent
- ❑ Bible
- ❑ Autres

33) Je voudrais participer a la mission, mais mon problème est (choisir une réponse)
a. _____ la Peur
b. _____ Langue
c. _____ l'argent
d. _____autres

34) Voici une liste d'article qui pourrait motiver les gens à être plus engagées à rejoindre les perdus. Choisir **quatre articles** par "M" pour ce qui motive le plus, et **quatre articles** par "L" pour ce qui vous motive le moins.

_____ Conférence Missionnaire

_____ Le sermon du Pasteur

_____ Les rapports missionnaires durant les services

_____ Les missionnaires invites a parler durant les services

_____ Un missionnaire me visitant a la maison

_____ Les lettres de prière des missionnaires

_____ Assister aux séminaires sur la mission

_____ Vidéos à m'aider à comprendre les problèmes sur le champ missionnaire.

_____ Assister a une étude Biblique sur la Grande Commission

35) Etes-vous un chrétien ___Oui   ___Non (choisir une réponse)

36) Depuis quand êtes vous en Amérique? (choisir une réponse)
- ❑ Moins d'un an
- ❑ 1 - 4 ans
- ❑ 5 – 10 ans
- ❑ Plus de 10 ans

37) Quel est votre âge? (Choisir une réponse)
- ❑ Au dessous de 12 ans
- ❑ 13 – 25 ans
- ❑ 26 – 38 ans
- ❑ 39 – 51 ans
- ❑ 52 ans et plus

38) Sexe: ___ Homme   ___Femme (choisir une réponse)

39) Je suis un chrétien (e) depuis
___0-5 ___6-10 ___11-15 ___16-21 ___ 22 et + (choisir une réponse)

40) J'assiste les services de cette église (choisir une réponse):

_____ chaque semaine

_____ deux fois par semaine

_____ chaque mois

_____ occasionnellement

_____ pour la première fois

41) Je suis né en: ___ Haïti _____ Aux Etats Unis d'Amérique _____Ailleurs
(choisir une réponse)

42) Je visite cette église ____ Oui ____ Non, et le nom de mon église
est_____

C'est tout. Merci de votre coopération !

APPENDIX 27: OUTLINE OF VIGCOM

VIGCOM
To Know the Great Commission and Make it Known

| Prayer | Preparation | Production | Publication | Proclamation |

Name of the Ministry: VIGCOM MINISTRIES

Vision: To know the Great Commission and make it known.

Mission: VIGCOM exists to motivate, mobilize and move ordinary people to the next level as to bring a contribution to the fulfillment of the Great Commission through Prayer, Preparation, Production, Publication, and Proclamation.

VIGCOM is a faith based ministry grounded in partnership with individuals, churches, and para-church organizations at different levels.

Core Values: **FACTS**

Faithful
Accountable
Commitment
Teachable
Sacrifice

For further information, visit www.vigcom.org

APPENDIX 28:
ABBREVIATIONS

AB	American Baptist
ABHMS	American Baptist Home Missionary Society
ABIS	American Bible Society
ABS	American Baptist Society
ACARP	Action Chrétienne a la recherché des âmes perdues
ACMC	Advancing Churches in Missions Commitment
AFAM	African American
AIM	African Inland Mission
APEHI	Association des Pasteurs Evangéliques Haïtiens D'Illinois
BGC	Baptist General Conference
BHM	Baptist Haiti Mission
CBH	Convention Baptiste Haitienne
CEEH	Concil des Eglises Evangéliques d'Haiti
CPM	Chosen People Ministries
CSI	Christian Service International
EBEFNY	Eglise Baptiste d'Expression Française de New York
EBM	Evangelical Baptist Missions
EBMB	Eglise Baptiste Missionnaire De Boston
EBPA	Eglise Biblique Pierre Angulaire
EBREF	Eglise Baptiste du Rédempteur d'Expression Française

EBT	Eglise Baptiste du Tabernacle
EBB	Eglise Baptiste de Bolosse
EDO	Eglise de Dieu d'Outremont
EEBB	Eglise Evangelique Baptiste Bethesda
EEBBF	Eglise Evangelique Baptiste Bethel (Florida)
EHG	Eglise Haitienne de la Grâce (CMA)
ELPB	Eglise La Bible Parle
EMIS	Evangelism and Missions Information Service
EMQ	Evangelical Missions Quarterly
FHBCO	First Haitian Baptist Church of Orlando
GBEUH	Groupe Biblique Des Etudiants et des Universitaires d'Haiti
HECA	Haitian Evangelistic Crusade Association
HGM	Heart of God Ministries
HMC	Haitian Missionary Church
IFES	International Fellowship of Evangelical Students
IFMA	Interdenominational Foreign Mission Association
IM	Interact Missions
LMM	Lumiere Medical Ministries
MEBSH	Mission Evangélique Baptiste du Sud D'Haiti
MEH	Mission Evangélique d'Haiti.
NEBM	Nouvelle Eglise Baptiste Missionnaire
NMBC	New Missionary Baptist Church
OMS	Oriental Missionary Society
SBC	Southern Baptist Convention
SDA	Seventh-Day Adventist

STEP	Séminaire de Théologie Evangélique de Port-au-Prince
TEE	Theological Education by Extension (programmes)
TM	Teach us Missions
UBS	Universal Bible Alliance
UCNH	Université Chrétienne Du Nord d'Haiti
UEBH	Union Evangélique Baptiste d'Haiti
UFM	Unevangelized Fields Mission
USAID	U.S. Agency for International Development
VGPMH	Vision Globale Du Protestantisme dans le Milieu Haitien (Global Vision for Protestantism in the Haitian Milieu)
VMM	Vision Missionnaire Mondiale
WEC	World Evangelism Crusade
WIM	West Indies Mission
WT	World Team